REMEMBERING
THE '40s

REMEMBERING THE '40s

A Decade in Words and Pictures

Nick Freeth

COMMISSIONING EDITOR: Will Steeds

EDITOR: Jo Richardson

DESIGNER: Philip Clucas MSIAD

COLOR REPRODUCTION: Berkeley Square

Printed and Bound in Spain

A SALAMANDER BOOK

Published by Salamander Books Ltd.,
8 Blenheim Court, Brewery Road,
London N7 9NY, United Kingdom.
A member of Chrysalis Books plc

© Salamander Books Ltd 2002

ISBN 1 84065 352 3

THE AUTHOR

Nick Freeth was born in London in 1956, and is a
graduate of St. Catharine's College, Cambridge. He
spent twelve years as a staffer at the BBC World Service,
where he specialized in making radio shows covering
folk, jazz, and blues, and has subsequently worked in
commercial broadcasting and as a freelance audio
producer. Nick has a long-standing fascination with
American culture: he is the co-author of four successful
books focusing on the development of the guitar in the
U.S.A., and his most recent publications include two
highly acclaimed guides to Route 66.

THE CONSULTANT

Bill Harris grew up in Northeastern Pennsylvania during
the 1940s and, as a teenager, moved with his family to
New York in 1949, eventually becoming a freelance
writer after a thirty-year career at *The New York Times*.
He has written sixteen books on various aspects of New
York history, including *Top of the World: The New New
York,* covering the period from the end of World War II
through the celebration of the new millennium. His
World Trade Center: A Tribute was a New York Times
best-seller.

Contents

Foreword 8–9

Prologue 10–17

CHAPTER ONE **Back Home** 18–27

CHAPTER TWO **On Main Street** 28–43

CHAPTER THREE **A Place of Our Own** 44–61

CHAPTER FOUR **At Work and School** 62–75

CHAPTER FIVE **That's Entertainment** 76–93

CHAPTER SIX **It's the Weekend** 94–113

CHAPTER SEVEN **On Stage and In Print** 114–123

CHAPTER EIGHT **Let's Go!** 124–137

How They Saw the Future 138–141

*Index, Bibliography,
and Acknowledgments* 142–144

Left: *Home again—World War II soldiers disembarking in New York after completing a gruelling European tour of duty. Some of them were subsequently to face further action in the fight against Japan.*

Foreword

It was like a giant crystal ball, two hundred feet in diameter, seemingly floating on fountains arrayed beneath it. But the "Perisphere," the symbol of the 1939 New York World's Fair, wasn't transparent. You had to go inside to see the future. What was in there was "Democracity," a representation of the city of the tomorrow, with satellite towns where people would actually live some day, and a network of highways that got them in and out through dazzling green countryside at speeds of a hundred miles an hour. People stood in long lines to see it, and when they came out they couldn't wait to get on to this wonderful "future."

That would be the 1940s. World War II came between them and their dreams, but the predictions started coming true just as soon as it was over over there. Maybe not quite in the same way that the Fair had promised, but Americans saw their lives change completely in the 1940s. Many of them moved to the suburbs. They weren't exactly as slick as Democracity's satellite towns, but you could see greenery from the windows of your Cape Cod cottage, split level, or ranch house. Your car strained to get up to sixty miles an hour, although the speedometer went up to one hundred.

The World's Fair had prepared Americans for a lot of the wonders ahead. It was the first time most of them had ever seen or heard of television. Computers weren't on anybody's wish list yet. The IBM pavilion was filled with an exhibition of fine art; and Remington Rand, who would develop the amazing Univac computer in the mid-1940s, devoted its building to electric shavers. They never got to buy a "Frig-O-Therm," a kitchen accessory that Frigidaire promised would cook a full meal and make ice cream for dessert at the same time. But the "Drug Store of Tomorrow," that predicted the corner drug store would soon be divided into self-service departments, kept its promise. U.S. Rubber hit the nail on the head, too, with its prediction that everybody would soon be wearing stretchable clothing made of "miracle yarns."

That wonderful world of the future that everybody so eagerly anticipated back in 1939 is buried deep in our past today. And some aspects of it may seem quaint compared to all of the futures that have come after it. But it was a great time be alive. You had the feeling that the world had gone about as far as it ever would. But then you'd wake up and find it had gone a little further while you were asleep. The American dream is all about futures.

But every now and then, it's fun to take a look back and see where we've been. That's what this book is all about. It describes a moment in America's history when, with the Great Depression and the war behind us, there was nowhere to go but up. It was an amazing moment.

BILL HARRIS

*Left: In this mid-1940s family scene, a mother and father
enjoy the pleasures of Christmas with their two young children.*

PROLOGUE

Victory!

"HURRAH!! HURRAH!! I'm COMING HOME!!! I may not be able to write again for a few days, so if my letters are rather scarce from now on for a while you'll know why. I have lots to do and little time to do it. I haven't even started to pack. Everything is A-OK. All of us are so happy we can hardly keep our feet on the ground. I am going to cut this short. Hope you'll forgive. SEE YOU REAL SOON!!"

KAY VOSS, U.S. EIGHTH AIR FORCE CO-PILOT, WRITING TO HIS PARENTS IN SUMMER, 1945, QUOTED IN THE GREATEST GENERATION SPEAKS BY TOM BROKAW

Within weeks of V-E Day, May 8, 1945, plans to return most American forces in Europe to the "Zone of the Interior" (as the U.S.A. was known in military jargon) had been finalized. Large-scale exoduses from airbases on British soil began the following month, with some personnel flying home via Iceland, and others crossing the Atlantic by ship.

Many servicemen, including the 381st Bombardment Group which arrived in New York on June 29, found themselves docking at the same piers from which they had set off for England at the start of the war, though the 381st's official history comments that "whereas [that departure] had been shrouded in silence and semi-secrecy, the homecoming was brightened by the mid-afternoon sunlight and enlivened by the screams of nearby craft and the musical welcome of good army bands in the harbor." Kay Voss was not among this early wave of returnees, but he made it home to Michigan by Labor Day—and was back at work behind the counter of his father's grocery store the very next morning!

Left: As the Allies' victory against Japan is announced, a sailor kisses a nurse in New York's Times Square. Similar spontaneous celebrations were soon taking place all over the country.

Right: Men of the Third Army's 86th Division (the Black Hawks), the first U.S. soldiers to return from Europe as a complete unit, cheering as they arrive in New York on June 17, 1945.

Those who had been stationed in the Pacific often had longer to wait
before demobilization, spending months occupying Japan in the wake of
the atomic explosions at Hiroshima and Nagasaki that ended the war
there. But for most other Americans, life—at a superficial level, at least—
swiftly returned to normal. Immediately after V-J Day (August 15, 1945),
restrictions on gasoline and the strictly imposed "Victory" speed limit of
thirty-five miles per hour were lifted. Soon factories were able to resume
the manufacture of luxury and consumer goods, and in 1947, the Office
of Price Administration, which had supervised rationing, was wound up.

Unlike other Allied economies (especially Britain's), America was in
excellent shape, and the struggles and losses of the war years, during
which nearly 300,000 of its citizens had been killed, served to strengthen
its resolve and dynamism in this new era of peace. The U.S.A.'s horizons
now seemed boundless, and its vigor and optimism unstoppable—in
sharp contrast to the scene only a few years earlier, when the nation had
faced the turn of the decade menaced by internal uncertainties and
divisions as well as by its potential enemies in Europe and Asia.

Below: London under attack: St. Paul's Cathedral stands proud amid the smoke and flames of the Blitz. The city was a major target for the German Luftwaffe's bombs during 1940 and 1941.

Right: A barber shop proprietor in London's St. Martin's Street opens for business after an air raid. The defiant signs on his boarded-up windows exemplify the courage and good humor that helped the capital survive the darkest days of the war.

1940

Temperatures around New York's Times Square had fallen ten degrees below zero by midnight on January 1, 1940, but neither the chill nor the threat of war in Europe could discourage the crowds of 1.25 million who saw in the decade there. Nevertheless, the anxieties undermining their celebrations were reflected in the day's broadcasts and newspaper editorials. New York Governor Herbert H. Lehman's radio address to the city contrasted the "peace and security that happily prevails in our own beloved country" with the "scene abroad...[where] millions of men and women have been deprived of freedom and the right to live as human beings," while *The New York Times*—which, like other leading U.S. papers, had been giving close coverage to recent events in Germany, Czechoslovakia, Poland, and Britain—observed that "though we are not in the war, we cannot avoid being in the crisis."

There was sharp controversy about whether—or to what extent—America should involve herself in a European conflict. Among the most extreme voices for isolationism was Father Charles E. Coughlin (1891–1979), a former supporter of President Franklin D. Roosevelt who had been infuriated by FDR's recognition of "the atheistic, godless government of the Communists in Russia," and was now taking an increasingly pro-Nazi, anti-Semitic line in his regular radio commentaries and through his "National Union for Social Justice."

More moderate U.S. opinion was also cautious about becoming embroiled in war, and the various Neutrality Acts that were passed during the 1930s effectively embargoed the provision of weapons to America's allies once they began fighting Germany and Italy. However, this legislation was modified in 1939, allowing the sale of some armaments. Roosevelt himself, "stretch[ing] his constitutional prerogatives to their outermost boundaries," in the words of historian David M. Kennedy, went on to win further ships and planes for France and Britain throughout 1940, the year that saw his election to an unprecedented third term in the White House. On December 29, during one of his celebrated "Fireside Chats" to the nation, FDR stressed his determination to continue supplying arms for "the war needs of Britain and the other free nations which are resisting aggression," and made his famous declaration that "we must be the great arsenal of democracy."

Meanwhile, press and radio accounts of events in Europe were providing graphic evidence of Nazi ruthlessness and violence, persuading growing numbers of Americans that war against Hitler was coming—and was justified. Of especial significance were the broadcasts of CBS correspondent Edward R. Murrow (1908–1965), whose dispatches from Blitz-torn London portrayed the realities of the horrific bombing campaign there with rare vividness and poignancy, but also conveyed the city's spirit of defiance. Following a heavy raid in September, 1940, Murrow reported that "I saw many flags flying from staffs. No one told these people to put out the flag. They simply feel like flying the Union Jack above their roof. And no flag up there was white."

Above: *President Franklin Delano Roosevelt (1882–1945), seen with his wife Eleanor and mother Sara (who died in 1941) in the library of his home in Hyde Park, New York. FDR broadcast several of his "Fireside Chats" (the first was heard in 1933) from this room.*

From Peace to War

In his State of the Union address on January 6, 1941, President Roosevelt enumerated the four key "human freedoms"—freedom of expression, freedom of worship, freedom from want, and freedom from fear—on which a secure international order should be based. He also warned his countrymen that the democratic way of life essential for the sustenance of these civilized values was "at this moment being directly assailed in every part of the world," and stressed the need to devote actions and policy "primarily—almost exclusively—to meeting this foreign peril."

In fact, plans to put America on a war-ready footing were already well advanced. The previous December, the Office of Production Management had been set up to coordinate the manufacture and supply of military hardware, and March, 1941 saw the passage of the "Lend-Lease" Bill, permitting the provision of ships and weaponry to allies such as Britain. Meanwhile, the nation's armed forces were growing in numbers and capability, thanks to substantial investment and the implementation of a selective draft (using peacetime conscription for the first time). By summer, 1941, the Army boasted 1.4 million men, while an article by Navy Secretary Frank Knox, published a few weeks before Pearl Harbor, claimed that America's sea-going defenders were now "the biggest, toughest, hardest-hitting, straightest-shooting in the world…primed and ready to write 'finis' to *Mein Kampf.*" Knox concluded, with a blast of almost hubristic defiance, "Let 'em come—from both sides, if they want to— we can win on two oceans!"

OURS...to fight for

FREEDOM FROM WANT

Above: One of a set of four posters featuring paintings specially created by Norman Rockwell (1894–1978) to illustrate the "four freedoms" proclaimed by Franklin D. Roosevelt in 1941. Rockwell's pictures were later used to promote the sale of war bonds.

America's failure to predict the date and location of Japan's sudden, devastating Hawaiian attack on December 7, 1941, despite a steady worsening Pacific crisis that had led Roosevelt to break off a vacation to return to Washington a few days previously, cost her dearly in lives and her sense of national security. But the actual transition from peace to war had been long prepared for, and it was accomplished calmly and efficiently. Extended conscription for men between the ages of twenty and forty-four was mandated on December 19. Rationing, initially affecting only automobile tires but subsequently extending to gasoline, food, and other essentials, swiftly followed, and householders were encouraged to grow their own produce and conserve or recycle precious resources. Used cooking fat could be put into cans and returned to butchers (it was an important ingredient in the manufacture of machine gun pellets), scrap rubber from women's girdles and garter belts was needed to produce Army trucks and other munitions, and there were even special regulations covering hunting—game was a valuable source not only of meat but of feathers for flying suits!

Such schemes were important but relatively small-scale. Only a massive redeployment of workers and resources could provide America and her allies with the supplies required to win the war, and the man- (and woman-) power to produce them. Bringing this about led to profound changes in the nation's industrial and social fabric.

Below: The destroyer USS Shaw at Pearl Harbor following the Japanese attack. After being given a new bow and bridge, she was able to resume active service in 1942.

Resolved by the Senate and House of Representatives of the ~~United~~ States of America in Congress assembled, That the state of ~~war~~ between the United States and the Imperial Government of ~~Jap~~an which has thus been thrust upon the United States is hereby ~~form~~ally declared; and the President is hereby authorized and ~~direc~~ted to employ the entire naval and military forces of the United ~~State~~s and the resources of the Government to carry on war against ~~the I~~mperial Government of Japan; and, to bring the conflict to a ~~success~~ful termination, all of the resources of the country are hereby ~~pledge~~d by the Congress of the United States.

Sam Rayburn

Speaker of the House of Representatives.

H A Wallace

Vice President of the United States and President of the Senate.

1941   4.10 p. m. E.S.T.

Roosevelt

Above and right: *In the wake of America's entry into World War II, thousands of young men were drafted into the armed forces. Our picture shows a group of new recruits being inducted at Camp Upton, NY.*

Above top: *Getting used to rationing— two young shoppers compare the prices and point values of canned and bottled fruit juices at their local grocery store.*

The Home Front

To produce planes, ships, tanks, guns, and the other necessities of war, America drew on its huge manufacturing capacity and unrivalled managerial expertise. There were ample government funds for defense contracts, guaranteed profits for the firms that undertook them, and excellent pay and overtime for employees, many of whom were lured away from farm jobs to industrial work that paid several times their former wages.

Below: Women aircraft workers at the Douglas plant in Long Beach, CA sign their names in lipstick on a newly completed bomber (nicknamed the "Memphis Belle") in August, 1943.

Some of these migrants were Southern blacks who flocked to centers of munitions production—especially to California, whose black population grew by approximately 250,000 during the war years. Their prospects were boosted by an Executive Order, dating from June, 1941, that outlawed racial discrimination in the defense industries. They formed a key part of the workforce producing "Liberty Ships" in Henry J. Kaiser's San Francisco Bay Area yards, and labored, further down the coast, in the massive aviation factories that earned Los Angeles the sobriquet "the Detroit of airplanes." By 1945, African-Americans comprised some 12 percent of federal employees, and in the following years, increasing numbers of them settled permanently in the Golden State.

Women were also vital to the war effort. A widely shown 1941 documentary, *Women In Defense* (scripted by Eleanor Roosevelt and narrated by Katharine Hepburn), described the contribution they were already making to science, volunteer services, and on the shop floor. It also showed them "assembling, gauging... riveting [and] drilling" in shipyards—an image soon to be promoted even more vigorously by the famous "Rosie the Riveter" campaign, which helped to encourage up to 19 million women into wartime employment. There, they worked alongside men (though rarely, at this stage, for equal pay) in almost every area of the defense industry. Former World War II

Left: A mushroom cloud rises above Nagasaki after the detonation of the plutonium bomb on August 9, 1945. The 10,000-pound device killed more than half the city's residents.

navigator Sam Halpert's memorable autobiographical novel, *A Real Good War* (1997), includes an account of his crew taking delivery of a new B-17 bomber, and finding, "tucked under the drift-meter gyro...a perfumed note with two lipsticked mouth prints and a message, Our Hearts Are With You Always—Drop One For Us—Mildred & Mary T.—Hydraulic Inspection."

To win the war, America maximized its industrial resources, switching thousands of civilian factories, including its Detroit automobile plants, to military production, and using ingenious manufacturing methods to make synthetic versions of essential materials, such as rubber, that were in short supply after Pearl Harbor. It also deployed a combination of existing technology and cutting-edge physics to create the nuclear weaponry that brought the war in Japan to its devastating conclusion.

Hydroelectric power from the Tennessee and Columbia Rivers was used to extract the uranium for "Little Boy," the Hiroshima bomb, and the plutonium for "Fat Man," which was dropped on Nagasaki. J. Robert Oppenheimer, the principal designer of both devices, was based, with his Manhattan Project colleagues, in makeshift laboratories in the New Mexico desert. After a successful test explosion on July 16, 1945, he responded to the awesome destructive power his twentieth-century science had unleashed by quoting a phrase from the ancient Hindu *Bhagavad-Gita*: "I am become Death, the shatterer of worlds."

Below: A recent recruit to Henry Kaiser's shipyards in Richmond, California, African-American trainee welder Josie Lucille Owens is seen here at work on the construction of a new Liberty Ship, the SS George Washington Carver.

Huge crowds attend New York City's Victory Parade on January 12, 1946.

BACK HOME

"The Capital of the World"

America and the United Nations

"It is my earnest hope, and indeed the hope of all mankind, that from this solemn occasion a better world shall emerge out of the blood and carnage of the past, a world founded upon faith and understanding, a world dedicated to the dignity of man and the fulfillment of his most cherished wish for freedom, tolerance, and justice."

GENERAL DOUGLAS MACARTHUR, DURING THE CEREMONY ABOARD THE USS MISSOURI ON SEPTEMBER 2, 1945, AT WHICH JAPAN FORMALLY SURRENDERED TO THE ALLIES

Having conquered Fascism, Allied leaders, and especially Americans, were eloquent in expressing their desire for security, peace, and justice at home and abroad. Among their greatest postwar triumphs was the establishment of an effective forum committed to the ideals of international cooperation and the avoidance of further armed conflict: the United Nations.

Franklin D. Roosevelt played a key role in creating the U.N.—even giving it its name—though he did not live to see it in operation. In the years following World War I, he had been strongly in favor of its predecessor, the League of Nations. But opposition in the Senate kept America out of the League, which later proved impotent against German and Japanese aggression. Roosevelt was eventually forced to acknowledge that it had become "nothing more than a debating society, and a poor one at that."

The basis for a better means of fostering global goodwill lay in the terms of the Atlantic Charter, signed on August 14, 1941 at Placentia Bay, Newfoundland by FDR and British Prime Minister Winston Churchill. This looked forward, "after the final destruction of the Nazi tyranny," to "a peace which will…[allow] all men…[to] live out their lives in freedom from fear and want." On January 1 the next year, a "Declaration by United Nations" (America, Britain, and, initially, twenty-four other countries) endorsed the principles set out in the Charter; by March, 1945, this document had gathered nineteen more signatories. The structure and operation of what was to become the United Nations Organization were finalized at a conference attended by representatives of the U.S.A., U.S.S.R., U.K., and China at Dumbarton Oaks, Washington in August, 1944, and at a summit between Roosevelt, Churchill, and Stalin at Yalta in

Left: *Winston Churchill, Franklin D. Roosevelt, Josef Stalin, and their aides photographed during the Yalta conference, held during February, 1945 at a palace on the Soviet Union's Black Sea once used by the Czars. It was to be the three leaders' last joint meeting—Roosevelt had barely two months left to live.*

June 22, 1944
President Roosevelt signs the "GI Bill of Rights" into law. It is designed to help veterans readjust to civilian life, and pays for them to enter higher education.

April 12, 1945
Death of Roosevelt; Harry S. Truman becomes 33rd President of the U.S.A.

May 8, 1945
V-E Day—the end of the war in Europe.

August 15, 1945
V-J Day—the end of the war with Japan.

June 26, 1945
Representatives of fifty countries sign the Charter of the United Nations in San Francisco. Following the ratification of the Charter by most of the signatories (and the addition of Poland to the list of original member states), the U.N. comes into being on October 24, 1945.

September, 1947
The House Un-American Activities Committee (H.U.A.C.), under the chairmanship of John Parnell Thomas, subpoenas forty-one witnesses at the start of its investigations into Communist influence on the movie industry. Hearings commence the following month.

April 3, 1948
President Truman signs the Economic Cooperation Act, based on proposals by Secretary of State George C. Marshall and his deputy, Dean Acheson, into law. The "Marshall Plan" provides wide-ranging financial support for European nations.

April 4, 1949
The U.S.A., U.K., and nine other nations (Belgium, Canada, France, Holland, Iceland, Italy, Luxembourg, Norway, and Portugal) sign the North Atlantic Treaty in Washington D.C. The North Atlantic Treaty Organization (NATO) is formally established on August 24 the same year.

February, 1945. Shortly before this second meeting, FDR had been elected to a fourth term as President. In his Inaugural Address he reminded his fellow Americans that "our own well-being is dependent on the well-being of other nations, far away…We have learned to be citizens of the world, members of the human community."

Just over ten weeks after Roosevelt's sudden death on April 12, 1945, the U.N. Charter was signed in San Francisco—a location widely favored as a permanent home for the new organization. However, the city's undoubted charms were brusquely dismissed by Soviet delegate Georgi Sakarin, who declared it "a second-rate place [that will] only attract second-rate diplomats." Philadelphia and Boston were also rejected, and New York was finally chosen as the site for the U.N. headquarters in December, 1946, making the Big Apple, in the eyes of many of its residents and visitors, the "Capital of the World." The General Assembly, Conference, and Secretariat Buildings, built on land in Manhattan donated by philanthropist John D. Rockefeller, Jr., and designed by a team of architects led by Wallace K. Harrison, were completed in 1952.

Above: The United Nations flag on display outside the organization's unfinished New York HQ in 1949.

Above: The nation mourns a great leader—women in Washington D.C. react to news of FDR's sudden death.

Rights and Racism

Below and below right: The GI Bill of Rights made it possible for the millions of Americans discharged from the armed services after the war to obtain funding for a college education. The textbooks held by the ex-soldier students in our photo (taken in 1945) were paid for out of annual grants of up to five hundred dollars per person, which also covered tuition fees and other costs.

Roosevelt's name is associated with many profoundly significant, painstakingly deliberated policies and initiatives. Yet one of his most influential pieces of legislation—a bill described by historian Michael Beschloss as having a "greater impact on bringing Americans into the middle class" than anything accomplished during the 1930s—was signed hurriedly, and without much publicity, just two weeks after D-Day. This was the Servicemen's Readjustment Act of 1944, better known as the GI Bill of Rights, guaranteeing state-funded higher education or training, low-interest property loans, and other benefits to all veterans who had served at least ninety days in the military after September 16, 1940. There was some opposition to the Bill in Congress and outside; many of its critics felt it over-generous to non-disabled ex-servicemen. However, both V.F.W. (Veterans of Foreign Wars) and American Legion lobbyists supported it vigorously, and one representative from Georgia, John Gibson, helped to sway the House in its favor by stating bluntly that "I'm here to lick anyone who tries to hold up the GI Bill of Rights. Americans are dying in Normandy."

C1906154   Series C

Honorable Discharge

from the

United States Navy

Above: A group of postwar Cadet Nurse Corps graduates photographed at Syracuse University, NY. With the students are Admiral Chester Nimitz and University Dean Edith Smith.

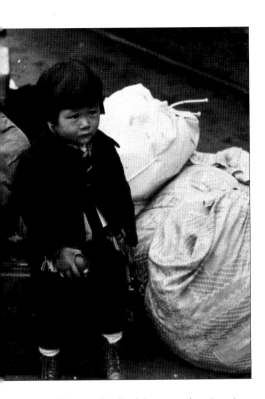

Above and right: A Japanese-American boy pictured in April, 1942 on the move from Los Angeles to an internment colony. Californians of Japanese descent (like the owner of this Oakland grocery store) were loyal U.S. citizens, but were powerless against the wartime decision to remove them from their homes and businesses.

The Readjustment Act remained in force until 1956, enabling over 2 million veterans to enrol in college, and giving many more the opportunity to learn a trade and buy their own house, farm, or business. Its importance to the development of postwar America is difficult to overstate, and is epitomized by the story of former serviceman Frank G. Nolte, told in Tom Brokaw's *The Greatest Generation Speaks* (1999): "I took advantage of the GI Bill, earned a graduate degree, and went on to teach at a community college for almost forty years. I traveled from a new home purchased on the GI Bill benefits and still live in it. No member of my family ever graduated from college [before me]."

While veterans had undoubtedly earned the preferential treatment afforded by their Bill of Rights, many other U.S. citizens were also in sore need of assistance and justice. The racism and bigotry against which the

Allies had fought so bravely in Europe, Asia, and Africa remained all too prevalent in some parts of America itself. Shortly before the end of the war, New York *Daily Mirror* journalist Walter Winchell asked a young Negro girl how she felt Hitler should be punished. Her reply was a stinging one: "Paint him black and bring him over here."

Discrimination also affected other minorities, notably the West Coast Japanese community, whose mass wartime internment on spurious security grounds was perhaps the most shameful action ever sanctioned by Roosevelt's administration. Harry Truman attempted to address the issue in December, 1946 by establishing a Presidential Commission to suggest "more adequate means and procedures for the protection of the civil rights of the people of the United States." Its findings, published the following October, were to lead to gradual improvements in this troubled area, and are examined later in this chapter.

Hawaii

Hawaii became a United States territory in 1898, and the outstanding natural beauty of its islands, as well as its distinctive music and culture, were soon to give it a unique place in the hearts of many Americans. Even before annexation, its special qualities were already widely known, thanks to the eloquence of visitors such as authors Mark Twain and Robert Louis Stevenson. Twain later commented that "No alien land in all the world has any deep, strong charm for me but that one; no other land could so longingly and beseechingly haunt me, sleeping and waking, through half a lifetime, as that one has done."

The early 1900s saw the start of organized tourism to the archipelago—and especially to Oahu, whose attractions included Waikiki Beach and Honolulu. The 1915 Panama Pacific Exhibition in San Francisco, which showcased dancers and musicians from the islands, gave Hawaii's profile a further boost. Subsequently, native performers such as steel guitarist Sol Hoopii became famous on the mainland, and by the 1930s, Hawaiian locations were being used in major movies like Bing Crosby's *Waikiki Wedding* (1937), which featured guest appearances by Hoopii and fellow guitarist Lani McIntire. Crosby was also one of the first American stars to wear an "aloha shirt." These colorful garments acquired their name in 1936 from local manufacturer Ellery J. Chun, and before long, Frank Sinatra and other luminaries would be sporting them on stage and screen.

In the meantime, however, Hawaii—though retaining its reputation as an exotic paradise—was to gain a more serious significance as a vital link in America's defenses. The U.S. naval base at Pearl Harbor in Oahu had been

Right: A group of vacationers enjoy a leisurely meal—and some exotic cocktails—at a restaurant beside Honolulu's Waikiki Beach in 1945. The setting is idyllic, and by the late 1940s, Hawaii was attracting record numbers of tourists—many of them taking advantage of improved air links from the American mainland.

established as long ago as 1908, but in spring, 1940 it became the home for much of the Pacific fleet and a prime target for the terrible events of the following December.

During the war years, the territory was a major base for service personnel, ships, ammunition, and aircraft, and martial law was imposed until 1944. Nevertheless, with the ending of hostilities—and despite the severe damage caused by a *tsunami* (tidal wave) that struck some of the islands on April 1, 1946, resulting in 149 deaths—tourists gradually began to come back. Their numbers were increased by the resumption of passenger services from California by the Matson shipping line, whose liner *Lurline*, fresh from a multi-million dollar refit after its earlier service as a troop transport, made a triumphant postwar return to Honolulu in spring, 1948.

That year, visitors to Hawaii reached almost 42,000—a record figure that boded well for the territory's future. One major disappointment for its citizens during this buoyant period was their continuing failure to be granted U.S. statehood, despite support from many leading American politicians, including President Harry Truman. In the end, Hawaii was not to enter the Union until 1959.

Above left: Frank Sinatra, resplendent in a fashionable shirt decorated with Hawaiian-style surfer figures, joins a more soberly attired Orson Welles on CBS's "Broadway Bandbox" in 1943.

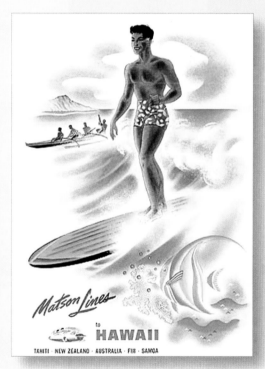

Above: The Matson line, synonymous with sea travel to Hawaii since the late nineteenth century, reintroduced its cruises to Honolulu after the war, and also served many other Pacific destinations.

America's Changing Mood

The 1947 report submitted to Harry Truman by the Presidential Commission that he had set up the previous year (see pages 22–23) took its title, *To Secure These Rights*, from the 1776 American Declaration of Independence. It recommended measures to outlaw discrimination against blacks in employment, education, and housing, and its appearance led to swift and significant legislative action—including Executive Order 9981, issued on July 26, 1948, proclaiming that "…there shall be equality of treatment and opportunity for all persons in the armed services without regard to race, color, religion, or national origin." In August, 1946, the Truman administration had faced up to another long-standing civil rights grievance by establishing the Indian Claims Commission—an independent agency charged with adjudicating claims from Native Americans relating to the loss of their ancestral lands. The same year saw a further victory against racism when the Supreme Court delivered its landmark verdict in *Morgan v. Virginia.*

A young black woman, Irene Morgan, was on a Greyhound bus heading from Virginia to Maryland when its driver told her to give up her seat—at the back of the vehicle, where black passengers were expected to sit—to a white traveler. Morgan's refusal to do so led to her ejection from the bus. She later pleaded not guilty to a charge of breaking Virginia's "Jim Crow" segregation law. Following her conviction, she appealed the verdict; her case, backed by the National Association for the Advancement of Colored People, eventually reached the Supreme Court, which ruled that Virginia's Jim Crow legislation represented an unfair restriction on interstate commerce. This judgment seriously challenged similar segregation laws, but did not immediately sweep them away. Some manifestations of Jim Crow were to persist well into the 1960s.

America had made undoubted progress on civil rights, but the country was being increasingly affected by a widespread mood of uneasiness— even paranoia. This was largely caused by concern over Communism, whose pervasive influence in many parts of Europe, and specifically in Greece

Right: President Truman is joined by two Native Americans as he signs legislation setting up the Indian Claims Commission.
Below: A branch office of the National Association for the Advancement of Colored People (N.A.A.C.P.), c. 1945.

H.U.A.C. and the "Enemy Within"

Russian Pressure: Basis for U.S. Aid to Turkey

Above: A diagram published in 1947, detailing the supplies and support given to Turkey by America in response to the threat from Communist Russia.

President Truman's 1947 "Loyalty Program" targeted suspect federal employees, but the notorious House Un-American Activities Committee (H.U.A.C.) had a much broader agenda. Before the war, the Committee, first convened in 1938 under the chairmanship of Martin Dies, had been zealous in its search for "front organizations," which it defined as groups "seek[ing] to undermine democracy and substitute dictatorship of whatever sort for it," and had accused several major trade unions of being "more than tinged with Communism."

However, in 1940, *The New York Times* took a sanguine view of H.U.A.C.'s findings, commenting that "Mr. Dies has been looking under every bed for Communists and Nazis, and has found some, but most of us are easy in our minds about them. They haven't been having the kind of advertising that appeals to Americans."

After 1945, H.U.A.C., now a permanent ("standing") House committee, redoubled its crusade against Communist subversion. It was less effective in seeking out extreme right-wing groups: John Gunther's *Inside U.S.A.* (1947) reveals that H.U.A.C. member John E. Rankin, a Mississippi Congressman, declined to investigate the Ku Klux Klan because it was, "after all, not 'Un-American' but 'American'."

and Turkey, provoked Truman's famous March, 1947 appeal to Congress for funds "to support free peoples who are resisting attempted subjugation by armed minorities or by outside pressures." The President's policies for containing a perceived Red Menace included the launch of initiatives with an overseas focus, like the Marshall Plan (designed to provide aid to Europe, but also to bolster U.S. interests there), and the creation of the Central Intelligence Agency. Meanwhile, life inside America was touched by a growing fear of possible "enemies within," and 1947's Executive Order 9835 sanctioned a probe of the "loyalty" of government employees, as well as the exposure of groups considered to be "totalitarian, fascist, Communist, or subversive."

During the next five years, this legislation was to lead to fruitless and destructive investigations into millions of innocent citizens.

Left: Alger Hiss (far right) leaves a New York court with his lawyers during his perjury trial in June, 1949. The jury later failed to agree on a verdict, but after a second trial, Hiss was found guilty and given a five-year jail sentence. He spent three years behind bars, and protested his innocence until his death in 1996.

Instead, H.U.A.C. focused on the exposure of former State Department official Alger Hiss, who was convicted of perjury in 1950 after his previous Communist activities (which he had denied) were revealed in evidence from journalist Whittaker Chambers; and—most famously—on an enquiry into the influence of Reds and "fellow-travelers" in the movie industry. This began in 1947, and led to ten "hostile witnesses" (nine Hollywood screenwriters and a director) being held in contempt by H.U.A.C. after refusing to answer questions about their past or current membership of the Communist Party. The "Hollywood Ten" went to jail for their silence, the studio bosses declared that they would not knowingly employ Party members, and the subsequent "blacklisting" of movie workers with supposed left-wing sympathies was soon to damage many more careers.

A deserted small town Main Street photographed in the depths of winter.

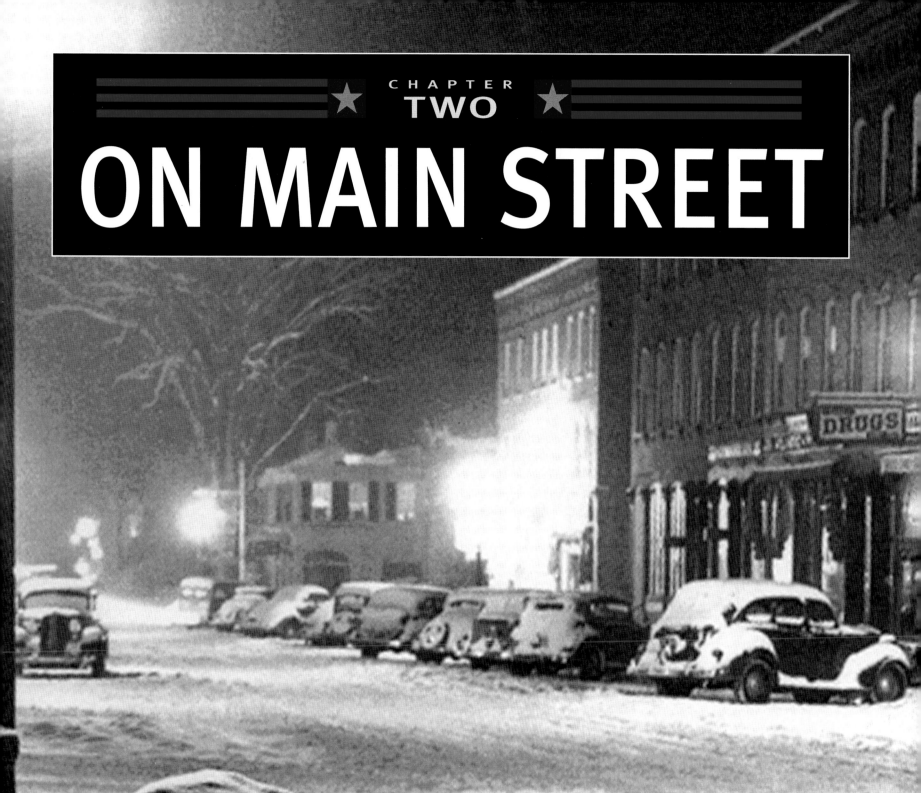

ON MAIN STREET

MAIN STREET

Gopher Prairie Revisited

"This is America—a town of a few thousand, in a region of wheat and corn and dairies and little groves. The town is, in our tale, called 'Gopher Prairie, Minnesota. But its Main Street is the continuation of Main Streets everywhere.

"The story would be the same in Ohio or Montana, in Kansas or Kentucky or Illinois… Main Street is the climax of civilization…Our railway station is the final aspiration of architecture. Sam Clark's annual hardware turnover is the envy of the four counties which constitute God's Country. In the sensitive art of the Rosebud Movie Palace there is a Message, and humor strictly moral. Such is our comfortable tradition and sure faith."

FROM THE OPENING OF MAIN STREET BY SINCLAIR LEWIS

Early in Sinclair Lewis' classic novel, *Main Street*, two characters give us their contrasting impressions of downtown Gopher Prairie. Carol Kennicott, a newcomer who has just married the local doctor, surveys Dyer's Drug Store, with its "greasy marble soda-fountain" and "pawed-over heaps of toothbrushes and combs," and sees a display of "black, overripe bananas and lettuce on which a cat was sleeping" in the local grocery store. She also takes in the sights and smells of Billy's Lunch: "Thick handleless cups on the wet oilcloth-covered counter. An odor of onions and the smoke of hot lard. In the doorway a young man audibly sucking a toothpick." Her verdict is damning: "In all the town there was not one building save the Ionic bank which gave pleasure to Carol's eyes; not a dozen buildings which suggested that…the citizens had realized that it was either desirable or possible to make this, their common home, amusing or attractive."

Gopher Prairie is much more pleasing to Bea Sorenson, a country girl who arrives in town on the same train as Carol, and is soon to become her servant. For her, Main Street is full of bustle and

Above left and right: Two postcard views of downtown Sauk Centre, Minnesota, birthplace of Sinclair Lewis and the inspiration for Gopher Prairie in his novel Main Street. The photo on the left dates from 1925 (just five years after the book was published), the one on the right from 1940.

MAIN STREET

opulence. She admires the drugstore's marble counter, and imagines having a date there, beneath the "glass shelves, and bottles of new kinds of soft drinks." The nearby movie theater offers different movies every evening—a far cry from the shows that came along every two weeks to the rural hamlet near her old home. And there are "four whole blocks" of stores, whose stock and decor, so tawdry in Carol's eyes, represent the last word in sophistication and luxury to Bea. She is a little intimidated by the traffic ("five automobuls on the street all at the same time—and one of 'em was a great big car that must of cost two thousand dollars"), but she concludes that it would be "worth while working for nothing, to be allowed to stay here."

Main Street was published in 1920, and Gopher Prairie was closely based on Sinclair Lewis' own birthplace, Sauk Centre, Minnesota. Shortly after the war, journalist John Gunther, researching his famous survey of 1940s America, *Inside U.S.A.*, visited the town and revealed how it had altered in the quarter century since Lewis described it. The drugstore was still there, as were a prewar bank and grocery store, but most of the old, wood-frame buildings, castigated by Carol for their "flimsy temporariness," had been replaced by brick structures. New businesses included a Chevrolet agency and a Ben Franklin craft store, and the appearance of other franchises and national chains was attracting more and more trade to Sauk Centre—much of it from the surrounding countryside, thanks to improvements in highway construction and a massive increase in automobile ownership. "Instead of being an outpost," wrote Gunther, the town had become "a pivot," even "a metropolis," and the same changes that had transformed it could be seen throughout the nation.

In the following pages, we take our own look at Main Street U.S.A., charting its development during the 1940s, and focusing on the goods and services it offered its customers. We also examine some of the challenges it was soon to face from suburban shopping sites, and from the road planners who threatened to divert traffic and business from downtown areas.

Above: This little drugstore, sited on the Main Street of Southington, Connecticut, was photographed by Fenno Jacobs in 1942. Its proprietress, Ethel Oxley, is shown surrounded by her impressive range of stock. As historian Spencer Crump has commented, "drugstores did much more than fill prescriptions during this era. They provided…cosmetics, film, candy, and miscellaneous gifts, [and] helped the customer by answering questions in detail [and] making suggestions."

1940s TIMELINE

1940
Average U.S. annual salary is $1,195; by the end of the decade it had risen to $2,543.

1942–1945
Most foods and vital commodities are rationed during the war years; ration books are first issued in May, 1942. Supplies of hard liquor are limited as distillers switch to making industrial alcohol for military purposes, though whiskey and other spirits produced before the outbreak of war are still available.

1944
Clarence Birdseye (1886–1956), whose company, Birdseye Seafoods, Inc., founded in 1924, pioneered the quick-freezing of fish, vegetables, and other food, introduces a U.S.-wide distribution system for his products using refrigerated railroad boxcars.

March, 1946
"Théâtre de la Mode" (Theater of Fashion) exhibition, featuring dolls wearing miniature versions of the latest in French haute couture, opens in New York. America's influential Women's Wear Daily is "well and truly stunned" by the collection, which has a significant influence on U.S. designers and retailers.

May, 1948
Paramount and other major Hollywood studios lose a key anti-trust case when the Supreme Court rules that their practice of distributing movies through their own chains of theaters has led to "price-fixing conspiracies." The companies are forced to sell off their theaters.

December, 1948
Brothers Dick and Maurice McDonald introduce a new "Speedee Service System" at their roadside restaurant in San Bernardino, California, creating the first "McDonald's" fast-food outlet.

Shopping on Main Street

In the 1940s, a town's main drag was a major thoroughfare, carrying both local and long-distance traffic; even state or national highways, like the famous Route 66 from Chicago to Los Angeles, would usually pass directly through the centers of urban communities in its path. This ensured a steady flow of customers to downtown businesses, many of which were small, privately owned concerns, operating in stiff competition to the numerous chain stores, run by large regionally or nationally based firms, that had already started to transform Main Street.

Most famous chains owed their success to the energy and commitment of individual entrepreneurs. Charles R. Walgreen, Sr. started out with a single drugstore in Dixon, Illinois in 1901; three decades later, he had built up an empire of over five hundred shops. F.W. Woolworth (described as "the worst salesman in the world" by an early employer) opened his first retail outlet in 1879; soon, Woolworth's was to become the nation's favorite "five-and-dime" (or "variety") store. And by the early 1930s, a New York-based tea importing company founded in 1859 by two partners, George F. Gilman and George H. Hartford, had transformed itself into the Atlantic and Pacific (A & P)—a nationwide grocery business recognized as the biggest retail chain in the world.

These firms' massive buying power and ability to offer bargain prices was widely resented by their locally based rivals. Several individual states imposed heavy taxes on chains, and in 1936 Congress passed the Robinson-Patman Act, an anti-monopoly measure designed to ensure that wholesale suppliers did not sell their goods more cheaply to big retailers. Despite such legislation, smaller companies still struggled to compete with the chains' shrewd marketing strategies. During the postwar years,

Above: Main Street, International Falls, Minnesota in 1945. Its local branch of Walgreens (left) boasts a colorful sign designed to attract the attention of both motorists and pedestrians.

Above top: A familiar store logo…A & P expanded steadily during the 1940s, and was also at the forefront of supermarket development.

Walgreens stole a march on its old-fashioned competitors by becoming the first national drugstore to convert all its premises to self-service operation, while in 1948, A & P attracted attention—and gave a substantial boost to its poultry sales—with its "Chicken of Tomorrow" contest, in which farmers were encouraged to breed birds with more breast meat.

Family-run neighborhood stores could rarely aspire to such bold measures, relying instead on their unique atmosphere and personal service to retain customer loyalty. Food journalist Andrea Halgrimson was born in Fargo, North Dakota in 1940; in a column for the city's newspaper, *The Forum*, she recalls her childhood visits to some of its "mom-and-pops":

"A certain smell infused these stores. They were small and close but the odor was of vegetables and meat and cans…The aisles were short and narrow so things were easily and quickly found. All of the people working there wore white aprons…The cash register was at a counter close to the front door. They were full-service stores with produce, a meat department, frozen products—just like the supermarkets only so much more manageable."

Such convenience—combined with choice and value—characterized not only the "mom-and-pops" but the whole Main Street shopping experience. An impressive variety of different stores could all be found within a few blocks of each other, and the downtown area also boasted a range of restaurants, diners, bars, and other places for patrons to find refreshment after they had finished making their purchases.

Right: This Main Street store in Ranchester, a town in the Big Horn Mountains area of Wyoming, serves as a gas station as well as a supplier of food, drugs, and candy! Mobil shield signs like the one seen here first appeared in the U.S.A. in the 1930s.

U.S.GOVERNMENT WARNS SUGAR HOARDERS

Price Administrator Henderson says:

"Those who have hoards of sugar should **STOP BUYING AND START USING UP THEIR STOCKS,** since they will not be permitted under the rationing plan to get more sugar until their supplies have been reduced to normal proportions"

Food on Main Street

The 1930s had seen the start of food and restaurant franchising—a trend soon to have a profound effect on where and how Americans ate out. Massachusetts-based businessman Howard Johnson pioneered the concept after the Wall Street Crash in 1929 prevented him from raising money to buy more premises. Instead, he licensed the Howard Johnson name to other proprietors, and supplied them with ingredients—a system that brought him substantial profits, and led to new "HoJos" springing up in roadside locations throughout the Eastern states. Recipes could be franchised, too, as Beverly and Rubye Osborne proved with "Chicken In The Rough." The Osbornes created this tasty dish (fried chicken served with shoestring potatoes, hot rolls, and a jug of honey) at their Oklahoma City restaurant in 1937, and went on to license it to scores of other eateries from Illinois to California.

However, franchising remained a novelty on Main Street in the 1940s; the vast majority of lunch counters, cafés, and diners were still independently run, and the advent of war temporarily ruled out further expansion by entrepreneurs like Johnson. Many restaurants faced hard times during this period, as they struggled to devise palatable menus using substitutes for rationed ingredients. Corn syrup or honey often replaced sugar, and novelties like baked rice and spinach casserole were served on meatless days. But when regular supplies were available, dining out could be both pleasurable and inexpensive. According to local historian Betty Tabor, a wartime loin of pork dinner at a restaurant in Johnstown, NY cost just forty-five cents, while customers at the Maze Hotel's Halloween party in nearby Fonda could enjoy roast turkey (and a cocktail) for a dollar.

After 1945, the fortunes of eateries took a dramatic turn for the better. The daily number of restaurant meals served in America soared from 20 million (prewar) to more than 60 million, and new dishes began to appear alongside perennial favorites such as chicken and hamburgers—including the deep-dish pizza, which originated at Chicago's Pizzeria Uno in 1943. Meanwhile, what was soon to be known as "fast food" was already available from an ever-growing number of outlets—its history is told in detail on pages 42–43.

Above: This colorful "golfing rooster" sign quickly became familiar across the Mid-West and Western states, as Beverly and Rubye Osborne's "Chicken in the Rough" caught on during the late '30s and '40s.

Right: Hungry customers enjoy a quick snack, while others wait for a seat, at the busy lunch counter of the People's Drug Store on G Street, Washington D.C., in July, 1942.

★

"Let's Have a Beer"

America's brewers had celebrated the end of Prohibition in 1933 with gusto; one company, Schlitz of Milwaukee, marked the occasion by air-freighting the first case of beer it produced after repeal to the White House! But liquor makers' hopes of an immediate boom in sales were soon disappointed; alcohol consumption rose only slowly in the following years, and by the early 1940s the industry was facing new restrictions and difficulties.

These were largely caused by wartime rationing. Barley, the brewers' staple grain, was in such short supply that it had to be combined with corn and rice. This brought an unfamiliar lightness of flavor to American beer, although drinkers quickly got used to the different taste, which has since become an accepted characteristic of many mass-market brews. Canned beer, first introduced by Krueger of New Jersey in 1935, was also withdrawn from the domestic market during the war years, and in 1943, brewers were made to devote 15 percent of their capacity to military-related manufacturing.

However, most of the larger firms

Above and top: The bartender has every reason to smile as his customers quench their thirst! His bar-room is decorated with sporting pictures; similar images were also used by brewers like Schoenling (see mats) to promote their beers.

survived these problems, and emerged strongly into the post-1945 era. Two Cincinnati-based companies, Burger and Hudepohl, acquired a substantial customer base among homecoming veterans after their beers were supplied to U.S. forces in the Pacific by the War Department. Anheuser-Busch of St. Louis, producer of Budweiser and Michelob, continued to dominate both the beer- and baker's yeast-making industries (it had diversified into yeast production during Prohibition). In 1947, Schlitz became the biggest beer producer in the world when it opened its massive new Milwaukee bottling house. Other top national brands included long-established names such as Miller, Coors, and Carling, whose famous advertising jingle, "Hey Mabel—Black Label!," launched in 1949, was soon to become a favorite with TV viewers.

The Rise of the Supermarket

Supermarkets were a natural progression from the self-service system pioneered in 1916 by Clarence Saunders at his Piggly Wiggly grocery store in Memphis. Other retailers had already attempted to streamline the food-shopping process: four years earlier, some A & Ps had become "cash and carry" outlets, reducing prices by cutting out home deliveries, and no longer providing customers with credit. But Saunders went several stages further; instead of being served by a counter clerk, his patrons simply took the goods they required from the shelves, placed them in baskets, and paid for their purchases at a checkout near the front of the store.

The Piggly Wiggly was highly successful, and Saunders went on to patent his approach and franchise it to other grocers. But shops like his were relatively small, and they could not offer the substantial discounts that earned the first true supermarket operator, Irish American Michael J. Cullen, the title of "the World's Greatest Price Breaker." Cullen opened his King Kullen Grocery Company in Queens, New York in 1930. Soon customers were flocking to pick up food bargains at his converted garage premises, and, according to the firm's publicity, "by 1936 there were seventeen King Kullen supermarkets doing approximately $6 million annually." Cullen's innovations were gradually adopted by the big national chains; during the late 1930s, both A & P and Safeway began converting to supermarket-style operation, providing their patrons with shopping carts (invented in 1937 by Sylvan Goldman of Oklahoma City's Standard Food Stores) as an alternative to baskets.

With their low prices, extensive advertising, and tendency to stock not just groceries but sidelines such as cosmetics and confectionery, supermarkets could have a devastating effect on other Main Street stores, and their stylish exteriors and colorful signs and logos often contrasted sharply with the drab frontages of the "mom-and-pops." However, as the 1940s progressed, their actual numbers decreased, as the chains began closing smaller supermarkets and replacing them with

Above left: A 1940s Safeway store in Sheridan, Wyoming.

Above right: This ad, published in 1949 by the U.S. Wheat Flour Institute, features favorite sandwiches chosen by Eleanor Roosevelt and other celebrities.

Right: A customer makes use of a shopping cart stroller as she chooses groceries in a mid-1940s supermarket.

Right: A flyer for the popular Food Fair store chain.

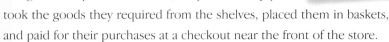

a few larger stores sited both downtown and (later) in suburban shopping malls, where access and parking were easier.

What supermarkets may have lacked in charm, individuality, and personal service, they made up for in convenience, value, and range—by 1950, a typical store stocked over 3,000 individual items. Before long, these brash newcomers to retailing had been accepted into the fabric of Main Street life, and had even become the stuff of poetry, as Allen Ginsberg demonstrated in *A Supermarket in California*:

"What peaches and what penumbras! Whole families shopping at night! Aisles full of husbands! Wives in the avocados, babies in the tomatoes!

…We strode down the open corridors together in our solitary fancy tasting artichokes, possessing every frozen delicacy, and never passing the cashier."

Below: Following the success of its first-ever retail outlet in Chicago, Sears built several more "flagship" stores in other major urban centers—like the one shown here, opened in 1941 in Baltimore, Maryland.

Left: A picture from the J.C. Penney archives, showing the exterior of a typical 1940s Penney store. The company, with its motto, "Honor, Confidence, Service, and Cooperation," was one of the most highly respected of all Main Street retailers.

Clothing Stores

Wartime rationing had an acute effect on both everyday clothing and high fashion: the government's L-85 "General Limitation Order," passed in 1942, specified exactly how much cloth could be used at hem- and waistlines, restricted the sizes and numbers of pleats and pockets, and prescribed a maximum height for the heels of ladies' shoes at one inch. To avoid unnecessary expense, women were encouraged to buy dresses suitable for day or evening wear, while men were unable to order an extra pair of pants with their suits, or to obtain shirts with French cuffs. Familiar fabrics like wool, silk, and even nylon were in short supply. They were sometimes replaced by what style specialist François Baudot describes as "more modest materials that had previously been regarded as unworthy of couture," such as Aralac (derived from milk protein) and rayon.

Main Street retailers rose readily to the challenges presented by this climate of austerity. In 1942, James Cash Penney, whose clothing store business, founded forty years previously in Kemmerer, Wyoming, now boasted over 1,500 outlets throughout America, stated that "thrift is nothing new to the Penney Company—it is our stock in trade." Penney's chief competitors, Montgomery Ward and Sears Roebuck, had an even longer tradition of offering value and service to their patrons, and were equally committed to providing garments that were as stylish and attractive as conditions allowed.

Ward had first sold clothing by mail order in 1872. Sears, originally a watch and jewelry dealer, launched its own general goods catalog twenty-four years later; it rapidly outstripped its rival, and had become a national institution by the 1920s. It enabled its customers to buy "cheap equivalent[s] of what 'smart' women were wearing in New York and Chicago," to quote journalist Alistair Cooke, as well as versions of clothes and accessories favored by early movie stars such as Clara Bow. Sears and Ward subsequently expanded into store ownership: the first Sears outlet opened in Chicago in 1925, and the company went on to establish a network of stores. It also had numerous catalog sales offices in smaller towns. Ward was to develop an even more prominent presence on Main Street, building up a chain of over five hundred department stores selling clothing and a wide range of household merchandise.

After the lifting of rationing in 1945, Montgomery Ward, Sears Roebuck, J.C. Penney, and other leading retailers were able to abandon the wartime "utility look" for more opulent and colorful designs. Over the next few years, their collections reflected, in a simplified and less expensive form, the latest trends in European *haute couture*, but were also influenced by the work of American designers, and retained some homegrown clothes that had established themselves earlier in the decade. These included the T-shirt, an item of military kit that was soon to become universally popular; women's pants, which were rarely seen before the war years; and denim jeans, formerly regarded solely as work garments, but now increasingly acceptable and even fashionable as casual wear.

Above: A crush of customers (including an enthusiastic looking sailor!) examine the range of ladies' stockings on sale at a branch of Montgomery Ward. Following wartime shortages, there was widespread demand for silk and nylon hosiery.

Movies on Main Street

The Rosebud, Gopher Prairie's wooden movie theater in Sinclair Lewis' *Main Street*, with its "lithographs announcing a film called 'Fatty In Love'" displayed outside, probably dated from about 1915—a time when theater construction was enjoying its first major boom. By the early 1920s, over 4,000 new picture palaces had opened. Within a few years, designers and proprietors were embarking on fresh flights of architectural fancy as the fashion for elaborate Art Deco theaters took hold, inspired by the French *Exposition Internationale des Arts Décoratifs et Industriels Modernes* that toured the U.S.A. in 1926. Some of these buildings succeeded in combining European, Spanish Colonial, and even Native American influences, like the two Boller Brothers theaters illustrated here.

The most magnificent Main Street theaters were usually the "first-run" houses where current films could be seen within weeks of their release. More humble outlets, such as the Rosebud, showed older movies, and often lacked the impressive facilities—pipe organs, liveried staff, and decor—of their upmarket cousins. Both types of theater were badly hit by the Depression, during which audiences dropped by a third, but their fortunes revived in the early 1940s, when up to 85 million Americans a week flocked to watch wartime newsreels and patriotic pictures, as well as classic movies such as *Casablanca* (1942) and *Double Indemnity* (1944).

The post-1945 period saw a gradual decline in Main Street movie attendance. This was largely due to the impact of television, although the movie industry suffered an additional blow in 1948, when the

Below and above right: Our main photo, taken in 1948, shows two rival movie theaters, the Granada and the State, on Main Street in Virginia, Minnesota. By the end of the decade, such picture houses were in hot competition with the drive-in theaters (like the one seen above) springing up on the outskirts of many towns, and packing in scores of motorized customers.

more and more customers. The drive-in concept had been conceived and patented by Richard M. Hollingshead, Jr. of Riverton, New Jersey in 1932, but "ozoners" (as they were sometimes termed) had initially been fairly slow to catch on. They owed their dramatic postwar success to a substantial growth in automobile ownership, and to an abundance of young, affluent patrons who relished the novelty of the new venues. For obvious reasons, drive-ins were especially popular with courting couples!

Above and below: The 1929 Coleman Theater in Miami, OK (above), and (below) the KiMo in Albuquerque, NM, dating from 1927. Both theaters were created by the leading Kansas City-based designers, Carl and Robert Boller.

Right and below right: Two drive-in patrons blissfully unconcerned with the movie on display. "Ozoners" sometimes screened major features like Billy Wilder's Double Indemnity, *but were more often associated with B-movies!*

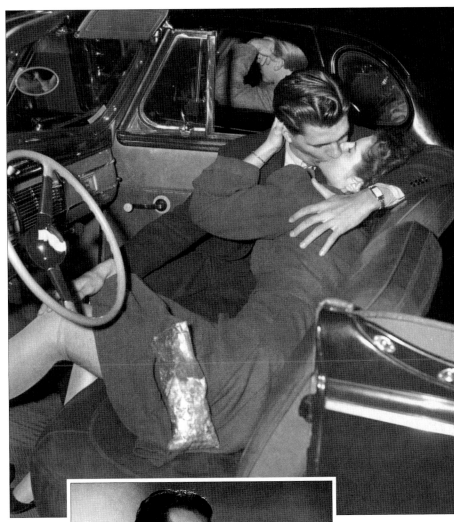

Department of Justice ruled that Hollywood's long-established control over film distribution and exhibition constituted an illegal monopoly. As film historian Mary Halnon explains, the major studios "were forced to divest their theaters, many of which could not survive as independents without Hollywood subsidy"; scores of them closed shortly afterward, including many large city-based houses.

However, as Main Street picture houses lost business, drive-in theaters, which were generally sited well away from town centers, were attracting

Decentralization

Kenneth Jackson's *Crabgrass Frontier: The Suburbanization of the United States* includes a comment made in 1926 by an Atlanta shopkeeper whose drugstore had recently closed: "A central location is no longer a good one for my sort of business…The place where trade is, is where automobiles go." At the time, not many other Main Street proprietors would have shared his pessimism. Cars ensured them a steady flow of potential customers, and although a handful of suburban shopping sites had sprung up (the first was probably the Country Club Plaza outside Kansas City, which opened in 1922), they seemed to pose little threat to the still-flourishing downtown areas.

By the late 1940s, however, it was clear that fewer people were coming into town for work, shopping, or leisure. In some places, the exodus had begun several years earlier. Robert M. Fogelson's *Downtown— Its Rise and Fall, 1880–1950* describes the sorry state of Chicago's business district at the start of the decade. Here, and in other city centers, obsolete office buildings were being torn down and replaced by parking lots, growing numbers of companies were moving out, and parts of downtown had become underpopulated and seedy.

Smaller towns were affected differently by the problems of decentralization. Highway traffic continued to flow up and down most Main Streets throughout the 1940s, keeping them lively and busy, though the advent of the Interstate system in 1956 was eventually to change this. But with postwar housing development expanding into ever more

Above: *The downtown area of Stroudsburg, Pennsylvania, pictured in 1946. Cars brought business to local stores, but also created parking and congestion problems. The ever-growing volume of traffic eventually led to the bypassing of urban centers by the 1950s interstate highways.*

outlying areas, dwellers in the new suburbs became increasingly divorced from downtown. Public transportation links between their distant neighborhoods and the main drag began to decline as automobile ownership soared, and the appearance of major chain stores like A & P and J.C. Penney in suburban shopping centers meant that regular trips into town were less essential. Despite these adverse conditions, many Main Streets succeeded in keeping a substantial proportion of their trade, especially in larger communities. But downtown businesses were never to regain their former, undisputed position at the heart of urban life.

Fast Food

The 1940s saw the birth of the modern "fast food" industry, although some of the cooking and promotional techniques associated with it had been developed several years earlier. In the 1930s, the White Castle hamburger chain, founded in Wichita, Kansas in 1921, was already deep-freezing its raw burger patties, running a coupon-based discount scheme for its customers, and using "trademark" storefronts and packaging to ensure that its premises and products stood out. During the same period, other firms, including Howard Johnson's (see pages 34–35), were siting their diners and sandwich stands on major highways to attract hungry travelers, and providing paper cups and plates for carry-out—polystyrene first appeared in the U.S.A. in 1938, but was not widely used in catering until the 1950s.

Above: The ultimate in self-service? This "Automat" on New York's Eighth Avenue dispenses plates containing cakes, pies, and other goodies at the drop of a coin.

After the war, many restaurant owners began looking for new ways to streamline their operations. Among them were two brothers, Dick and Maurice ("Mac") McDonald, the proprietors of a thriving eatery in San Bernadino, California. It offered an extensive menu, but needed a large staff to prepare food and bring it out to customers in cars. The McDonalds eventually realized that the most popular foods they sold were hamburgers and fries. In 1948 they launched their revolutionary "Speedee Service System," eliminating most other items from the bill of fare, cutting out the carhops, and instituting a factory-style cooking process that allowed orders to be filled as soon as they were placed. These methods, soon adopted by rival fast-food outlets, formed the basis for McDonald's subsequent national and global dominance; Dick and Maurice went on to sell their business to entrepreneur Ray Kroc for $2.7 million in 1961.

Above left: A young woman savors the hot dog she has just purchased from a stall at Palisades Park, New Jersey, in 1949.

Left: A carhop delivering snacks to motorists at an early 1940s drive-in. Fast-food provision would soon be streamlined by new cooking and serving methods devised by entrepreneurs like the McDonald brothers.

Rows of early 1940s tract houses at Strawberry Manor, California.

A PLACE OF OUR OWN

Housing

From Depression to Boom

"It takes a heap o' livin' in a house t' make it home,

A heap o' sun an' shadder, an' ye sometimes have t' roam

Afore ye really 'preciate the things ye lef' behind,

An' hunger fer 'em somehow, with 'em allus on yer mind.

It don't make any differunce how rich ye get t' be,

How much yer chairs an' tables cost, how great yer luxury;

It ain't home t' ye, though it be the palace of a king,

Until somehow yer soul is sort o' wrapped round everything..."

FROM HOME BY EDGAR A. GUEST (1881–1959)

Edgar A. Guest's sentimental poem about the "sun an' shadder" of home life would have been familiar to countless Americans—he was a widely syndicated columnist, and later a successful radio and television broadcaster—but for most of them, actually owning a house or apartment was an impossibility until the New Deal era. Many existing homeowners were dispossessed during the Depression, despite measures like Herbert Hoover's Federal Home Loan Bank Act, passed in 1932 in an attempt to increase the availability of mortgage funds, and prevent what the President, in his memoirs, described as "a million repetitions…[of] the poignant American drama revolving around the loss of the old homestead."

Franklin D. Roosevelt replaced Hoover at the White House the following year; among the legislation he introduced during his first hundred days in office was the Home Owners Refinancing Act, which provided additional loans to struggling mortgage holders. 1934 saw the setting up of the Federal Housing Administration (F.H.A.), a body that oversaw a fundamental change in mortgage terms and conditions. Previously, homebuyers had only been able to take out short-term loans—typically three to five years, although this was extended to fifteen by the Home Owners Refinancing Act. The F.H.A. inaugurated twenty-year (and later thirty-year) mortgage periods, raised the proportion of the property value that the loan could cover, fixed a standard 20 percent down-payment, and undertook to compensate lenders with government bonds if the borrower defaulted.

Other New Deal initiatives included the Wagner-Steagall National Housing Act of 1937, providing $500 million for public housing and

Above: Planning homes for heroes: a group of officials, including Presidential advisor Wilson W. Wyatt (second left), at the launch of a 1946 scheme to house war veterans in Maryland.

Left: Despite the demolition of some slum properties, much sub-standard accommodation remained in use in the 1940s—like this ramshackle Chicago lodging house, photographed in 1941.

Below: Thanks to postwar housing developments, more and more Americans could soon aspire to a home —and a front lawn—of their own!

instigating widespread slum clearances, and the creation of the 1938 Federal National Mortgage Association. Its function, in the words of home finance expert Chet Boddy, was "to buy...F.H.A.-insured mortgages from banks and other loan originators so [these] lenders would have a steady supply of money to make more loans," and its acronym quickly led to the affectionate nickname "Fannie Mae."

Such measures were designed not only to assist existing and potential homeowners, but also to boost the nation's building trade, which had already seen the loss of more than 2 million jobs. As historian David M. Kennedy comments in his Pulitzer Prize-winning study of the 1929–1945 period, *Freedom From Fear*, their initial success was limited: "The F.H.A. and Fannie Mae...neither built houses nor loaned money, nor did they manage to stimulate much new construction in the 1930s. However, they arranged an institutional landscape in which unprecedented amounts of private capital could flow into the home construction industry in the post-World War II years."

This investment was to prove vital after 1945, as an acute housing shortage, combined with an economic upturn, led to a massive demand for new homes. Entrepreneurs like the Levitt brothers (featured on pages 50–51) and American Community Builders, who created Park Forest, the "GI-town" south of Chicago, responded by producing properties that were plentiful, comfortable, and reasonably priced. But their bland uniformity was to upset some aesthetes, and the racism that excluded African-Americans from many developments was a sad betrayal of the goals set by the Housing Act of 1949, which called for "a decent home and a suitable living environment for every American family."

1940s TIMELINE

1934
Federal Housing Administration (F.H.A.) is set up. It provides insurance for mortgage lenders against defaults by borrowers.

1938
Federal National Mortgage Association ("Fannie Mae") is launched.

1940
43.6 percent of Americans are homeowners.

1944
Servicemen's Readjustment Act (GI Bill of Rights) provides favorable mortgage terms to veterans.

September 6, 1945
In a message to Congress, President Harry Truman states that "The largest single opportunity for the rapid postwar expansion of private investment and employment lies in the field of housing, both urban and rural...There is wide agreement that, over the next ten years, there should be built in the United States an average of from a million to a million and a half homes a year."

1947
The first Levittown opens on Hempstead Plains, Long Island; it will eventually boast over 17,000 homes.

1948
The U.S. Supreme Court rules in the case of *Shelley v. Kraemer*, finding that a restrictive covenant barring the transfer of a parcel of land in Missouri to a black family (the Shelleys) because of their color cannot be upheld in state or federal courts, and allowing the Shelleys title to the land.

1950
1,692,000 new homes are completed in a single year; 55 percent of Americans are now owner-occupiers.

Town and Country Housing

"What will life be like after Victory?" enquired a newspaper ad in early 1945. Featuring an artist's impression of an elegant family home designed by D. Allen Wright and fitted with a Silent Automatic Oil Heating system developed by the Timken company of Detroit, it invited readers to "picture [themselves] in this setting of health and happiness without a worry in the world." The house boasted two bedrooms, two bathrooms, large living and dining areas, and a "streamlined mechanical kitchen." The ad was coy about its actual price, but reassured would-be purchasers that "your War Bonds will pay a goodly portion of the cost," and concluded that "a home like this will be within the reach of everyone with a postwar income of $3,500 or more."

Even during the war years, well-heeled purchasers enjoyed an extensive choice of housing options and locations. For those weary of city life, buying a country home was an attractive possibility—although the process could be fraught with pitfalls, as humorist S.J. Perelman revealed in his story *Acres and Pains*, which includes this hilarious verbal demolition of the narrator's newly acquired rural hideaway by a visiting neighbor. "'Putty's rotten,' he said triumphantly. 'It's the talk of the countryside. And that's not all. See that stream down there? Every spring it rises to the second story. You'll be doubled up with rheumatism, if the mosquitoes don't get you first. You know, I never saw the shack by daylight before; no wonder they say it's haunted...'"

Perelman's fictitious farmstead was located in Pennsylvania, but throughout the Southern states, country dwellers, especially subsistence-level sharecroppers, faced hardships that were no laughing matter. Just after the war, John Gunther visited two tenant farms in Georgia, and later described what he saw there in his book *Inside U.S.A.*

Left: 1940s sharecroppers like this man often lacked adequate housing for themselves and their families.

Above: Prefabricated structures like this Quonset were home to thousands of munitions workers during World War II.

Below: A promise of prosperity in a postwar advertisement, which also warns its readers to safeguard the liberties on which their hopes and aspirations are based.

Above: The cramped interior of a postwar trailer home. Its occupants are a former soldier and his wife and daughter unable to find more suitable accommodation. Young families like these were among the principal targets for the new housing developments that were soon to emerge.

Neither house had running water or electricity; the first one, owned by a white farmer, was "propped up on lumps of rock," and the other, a two-room structure occupied by a Negro with ten children, was likened by Gunther to buildings he had seen "in the downfallen villages of Paraguay…and in some remote and utterly destitute areas in India."

It was little wonder that agricultural workers sought to escape these conditions by relocating to centers of wartime armaments manufacturing. The accommodation there was often spartan—trailers and prefabricated buildings were widely used—but it would have seemed luxurious in comparison to what they had left behind, and in time, some war workers were able to acquire better, more permanent homes. Substantial

numbers of such properties were built on the West Coast and elsewhere; they sold for about $4,000, and could be bought with the help of an F.H.A.-insured mortgage, or rented for as little as $40 a month.

But even these construction programs were insufficient to meet the huge postwar demand for housing. According to historian Gregory C. Randall, homecoming servicemen and their families, many of whom had never previously lived together, were often forced to stay "with relatives and friends and in make-do structures. Some were even living in chicken coops." They urgently needed new, adequate homes, and the design and building methods pioneered by developers like William and Alfred Levitt were soon to provide them in significant quantities.

Levittown

William Levitt (1907–1994) was a son of a New York attorney. In his early twenties, he went into business with his father and younger brother Alfred, supervising the construction of forty houses at Manhasset, on Long Island, and becoming President of the family-based firm, Levitt and Sons, which was set up shortly afterward. Despite the Depression, the company prospered, and, in 1941, it won a major contract to provide homes for defense workers in Norfolk, Virginia. Bill Levitt spent the war years as a lieutenant in the U.S. Navy's Construction Battalion (the Seabees), absorbing and applying their swift, highly disciplined building methods while serving in the Pacific.

On his return, Levitt and Sons began making plans for a highly ambitious venture: the creation of a sizeable new suburb on 6,000 acres of farmland east of the Long Island town of Hempstead. Levittown, as it was eventually named, comprised over 17,000 homes, together with stores, leisure facilities, churches, and synagogues. Building began on July 1, 1947, and three months later, three hundred of the site's Cape Cod-style houses were ready for occupation. Alfred Levitt designed these compact, two-story, two-bedroom units, but Bill masterminded their construction—a twenty-seven-stage process that he once likened to an "outdoor assembly line." The Levitts' efficient methods and economies of scale enabled them to sell their properties at attractive prices. Levittown homes cost just $7,500 when they first went on the market in 1948 (initially, they were only available for rent), and, thanks to the F.H.A. and the GI Bill, veterans could buy them with long-term, low-interest mortgages.

Right: The Long Island Levittown seen from the air in April, 1949. By the end of the year, Bill Levitt and his family had completed 10,000 houses there. Initial rentals and sales were exclusively to ex-servicemen, who could secure a Levitt home for a down-payment of just ninety dollars, and a monthly mortgage of fifty-eight dollars.

Below: Levittown developments were designed, from the outset, as complete communities. Shopping centers, parking lots, and other amenities were all located within easy reach of the houses, while trees and outdoor seating provided what one 1949 newspaper described as "charm and convenience."

Left: Leisure facilities at the Long Island Levittown included two athletic fields, no less than sixteen bowling alleys, and two swimming pools, one of which is seen under construction in this photo, taken in May, 1949. A group of residents' children eagerly watches the work in progress!

The Levitts were not the sole producers of cheap postwar housing; other notable developments included Park Forest, outside Chicago, which opened in 1948, and the many thousands of "Wherry" homes (named for the Nebraska senator who introduced the legislation that created them) built for the families of military personnel. But the Long Island Levittown, with its 82,000 residents, was the biggest—and most famous—project of its kind ever undertaken by a private contractor, and the family's approach to designing new communities (as well as their regrettable refusal to allow blacks to reside in them) was widely imitated. In 1949, Bill and Alfred launched a new, slightly larger style of home, the "Ranch," and the following decade saw the appearance of two further Levittowns—one in southeastern Pennsylvania, and the other at Willingboro, New Jersey.

The Living Room

The living room was sited at the front of Levittown houses and other typical 1940s properties, allowing parents to keep a watchful eye on children playing in the street outside. Its contents and layout also reflected a concern for child safety. Homes like the original Levitt Cape Cods, built on slabs of just twenty-five by thirty feet, offered little space for large families, and it was inevitable that kids would want to bring their toys (and occasionally rowdy games) into the living room. Therefore, furnishings and fittings needed to be robust and hazard-free, as well as comfortable and pleasing to adults.

Some manufacturers had ingenious suggestions on how to achieve this balance. In 1945, the Armstrong linoleum company launched a series of magazine ads demonstrating how its products could enhance homes, stores, and restaurants; one of them featured a list of "Ten ways to 'play-proof' a living room." Unsurprisingly, a few of these involved the use of linoleum on floor and table surfaces, but other ideas included the adoption of ceiling-suspended lighting (to avoid trailing flex), raising the level of the fireplace, slip-covering furniture in mohair ("hard to damage, easy to clean"), and installing the family radio and phonograph in a sunken cabinet. The results, displayed in a full-color artist's impression, were undoubtedly stylish, and the campaign proved highly influential.

However, the look of the "typical" living room in the Armstrong illustration was to change significantly over the following years, as a number of new-style furnishings made their way to the mass market. Perhaps the most important and enduring of these were the chair designs created by Charles Eames (1907–1978) with his wife Ray (1912–1988), and manufactured by the Herman Miller Company. The Eameses used a variety

Above: Companies like Magnavox excelled at enclosing television receivers and other domestic electronics in elegant wooden cabinets that "harmonized" with other living room furnishings. Significantly, some of the TV viewers in this ad are craning forward—few 1940s sets had screens bigger than ten inches.

of materials—fiberglass reinforced plastic, wire mesh, aluminum, and, most famously, molded plywood—for their seating. It required no upholstery, though it was sometimes supplied with leather, fabric, or calfskin coverings, and was easy and inexpensive to make. Their first plywood chair, which appeared in 1946, was a best-seller, and their furniture soon became a familiar sight in many American homes and offices. More conventional easy chairs and sofas were widely available from other companies, often for as little as sixty dollars.

The living room was also being graced by new electronic appliances. The Armstrong lounge had no television; set manufacture had been suspended during the war years, but before long, millions of TVs were coming off the production lines and being snapped up by eager would-be viewers. By the end of the decade, the Levitts and other developers were providing built-in receivers in all their homes, and "the box in the corner" was well on its way to becoming the focal point of many living rooms.

Meanwhile, the old, 78 rpm phonograph was under threat from two competing technologies. In 1948, Columbia introduced the first 12-inch vinylite long-playing records. These were virtually unbreakable, unlike the brittle shellac 78s, and able to accommodate up to fifty minutes of music. For obvious reasons, LPs appealed mainly to classical music lovers, but the following year, Columbia's rivals, RCA, launched a second disc format aimed at pop fans—the 45 rpm, 7-inch single, which could carry only one song per side. For several years, separate phonographs were needed to play each type of record; two- and three-speed machines only became available in the 1950s, when the manufacturers decided to bury their differences and allow their 7- and 12-inch discs to co-exist.

Husbands may have taken the lead in purchasing and operating such electrical gadgetry, but the choice of furniture and living room color schemes was usually made by the lady of the house—to whom, significantly, large numbers of home-related ads were directly addressed. Though some 19 million American women had full-time jobs by 1945, many others gave up paid employment after the war years, and, in the words of Joyce Cheney, author of *Aprons: Icons of the American Home*, "refocused their energy to create the idyllic concept of Home Sweet Home. It was something they could control; they applied themselves and excelled." However, this search for domestic perfection was combined with a down-to-earth refusal to become enslaved by housework and other chores. The ideal 1940s living room was bright, friendly, and cozy, but—like the other interiors featured in this chapter— it was also uncluttered, practical, and easy to clean and maintain.

Above: *A 1949 chair by Charles Eames. Its elegantly futuristic appearance is quite a departure from Eames' earlier, more straightforward home and office furnishings, and would have appealed to householders seeking the latest and best in contemporary seating design.*

Right: *Somewhat simpler, cheaper seating can be seen in this living room —part of the 1946 Maryland housing development whose launch was illustrated on page 47. The dwellings shown here had originally been used by war workers in Connecticut, but were subsequently shipped to Silver Springs, Maryland, and reassembled to create homes for veterans and their families.*

The Kitchen

In many ways, the kitchen, which usually incorporated a small dining or breakfasting area, was the heart of the 1940s home. It also sported an impressive concentration of technology designed to ease the daily chores of food preparation and laundry. Washing machines, supplied as standard in most new houses and installed in the kitchen or a nearby closet, were becoming ubiquitous, while postwar stoves and refrigerators boasted a variety of innovative and powerful features.

Refrigerators had evolved from the insulated wooden boxes, kept cold by regular deliveries of ice blocks, used by numerous households until the 1930s. Early electric models were small and unsuitable for long-term frozen food storage, but by the 1940s, their capacity had greatly increased, and they now included salad crispers, separate meat lockers, and adjustable shelving. Gas, promoted by the American Gas Corporation as "the wonder flame that cools as well as heats," was also widely used to power refrigerators, and gas-fired cookers and stoves—often fitted with extras like automatic timers and special toasting and barbecuing compartments—were preferred to

their electric counterparts by many housewives. The first microwave ovens went on sale in 1947, but they were bulky and expensive (over $2,000), and it took decades for them to gain a place in home kitchens.

Other new developments caught on much more quickly. Stainless steel was introduced just after World War II, and was soon being used for sinks (previously made from porcelain, earthenware, or Monel) and worktops. And at about the same time, Tupperware made its domestic debut. New Hampshire-based inventor Earl Tupper had created his first plastic containers in the early 1940s, but the product owed much of its subsequent success to Brownie Wise, the woman hired by Earl in 1948 to promote it. Ms. Wise went on to devise the "Tupperware party"—a direct-selling operation that was to transform Tupper and his unassuming but highly practical utensils into true household names.

Above: A typical 1940s fitted kitchen, in which almost every inch of available space is ingeniously used to accommodate appliances or provide work surfaces and storage. The housewife can even sit down while doing the washing-up!

Above right: In this 1947 ad, a saleswoman shows off an array of Westinghouse kitchen equipment, including an iron, a waffle baker (center), and an electric egg beater.

Right: "Now that's clean!"—a late 1940s advertisement demonstrates the capabilities of an electric dishwasher.

On the Kitchen Shelf

Many of the food brands found in the 1940s kitchen are still familiar to us today, although some of them took on a special significance during the war years. Catsups and sauces were widely promoted as "meat stretchers" that would make rationed ingredients go further, and Spam, which was more freely available than fresh meats, became a best-selling staple.

Other 1940s favorites included canned foods by Heinz and Campbell's (Campbell's added "Cream of Chicken" to its famous range of condensed soups in 1947), as well as cereals like Kellogg's Corn Flakes, Nabisco Shredded Wheat, and Wheaties—introduced by the Washburn Crosby Company (later General Mills) in 1924, and known as "The Breakfast of Champions" through its manufacturer's sponsorship of baseball broadcasts. Among the Wheaties sportscasters was the young Ronald Reagan, who was soon to be associated with a second famous brand—in 1948, he and other star names helped to launch Campbell's new V8 tomato juice.

Another celebrity food endorsee, Betty Crocker, was not quite all she seemed. Washburn Crosby invented the Crocker character in 1921 to promote its flour products and answer customers' letters. "Betty" went on to become a broadcaster, and in 1945, a survey voted her the nation's "First Lady of Food." Two years later, her name graced America's first-ever packaged cake mix, Betty Crocker's Ginger Cake; it was subsequently to appear on a wide range of other popular foods and cookbooks.

Right: An ever popular brand…Heinz tomato ketchup first appeared in 1876. The firm's founder, Henry J. Heinz of Pittsburgh, had gone into business seven years earlier; he introduced his "57 varieties" slogan in 1892.

Above: Betty Crocker's Ginger Cake mix was soon joined on the shelves by similarly pre-packaged ingredients for Party Cake and Devil's Food Cake—all designed, as one ad put it, to yield "lighter, more luscious" results from home baking.

The Bathroom

1929 saw the publication of actor and vaudevillian Charles ("Chic") Sale's comic monologue *The Specialist*, in which Lem Putt, self-proclaimed "champion privybuilder of Sangamon County," shares the fruits of a lifetime's experience in sanitation with his audience. Lem explains the drawbacks of making the seats in his outdoor conveniences over-comfortable (farmhands will spend too long sitting on them), advises a potential customer on privy location ("her being near a tree is bad. There ain't no sound in nature so disconcertin' as the sound of apples droppin' on th' roof"), recommends the use of substantial door latches ("with a hook and eye she's yours, you might say, for the whole afternoon"), and emphasizes the need for adequate excavation before construction begins ("It's a mighty sight better to have a little privy over a big hole than a big privy over a little hole"). He also waxes indignant about the use of insufficiently absorbent color sheets in the mail-order catalogs that hang in his outhouses: "Somethin' really ought to be done about this, and I've thought about takin' it up with Mr. Sears Roebuck hisself."

Sale's book sold over 2 million copies, and retained its popularity for decades, although by the 1940s, there would have been a declining demand for the special skills of men like Lem Putt. Indoor plumbing was becoming more common (even in remote rural areas), the production of enameled fixtures had grown rapidly throughout the previous twenty years, and, in the words of academic Ruth Schwartz Cowan, "the standard American bathroom had achieved its standard American form: the recessed tub, plus tiled floors and walls…a single-unit toilet, [a] sink, and a medicine chest, all set into a small room which was very often five feet square."

However, modern-style bathrooms and lavatories were not yet ubiquitous. At the start of the decade, according to figures quoted recently by the *Washington Post*, 13 million American homes were still without flush toilets, while 16 million had no bath or shower.

Above: *Charles Sale's book* The Specialist.

[28]

When we gets to the top of the hill

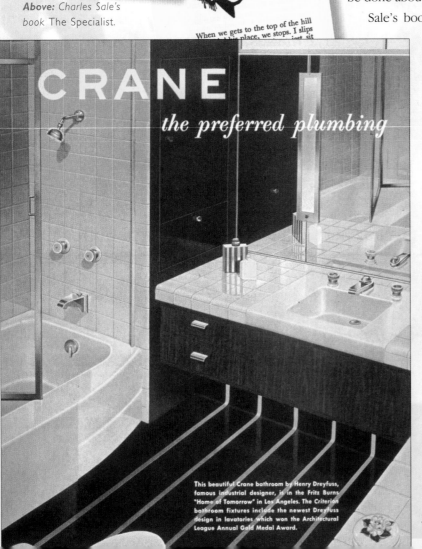

Left: *Small but well-equipped bathrooms like this one were found in many postwar American homes, although the stylish bath and basin units are a little more elaborate than the more basic fittings supplied as standard by builders such as the Levitts.*

CRANE

the preferred plumbing

This beautiful Crane bathroom by Henry Dreyfuss, famous industrial designer, is in the Fritz Burns "Home of Tomorrow" in Los Angeles. The Criterion bathroom fixtures include the newest Dreyfuss design in lavatories which won the Architectural League Annual Gold Medal Award.

THE SCOTTISSUE TWINS—A PERFECT PA

Softie   Toughie

Twin Qualities essential in toilet tissue…
SOFTNESS and TOUGHNESS

Left: An ad for a leading brand of toilet tissue, whose "linen-like" gentleness was far superior to that of the old catalog pages once used in America's privies!

Above: The joys of cleanliness—most new 1940s houses had ample hot water for daily showers and baths. (Note the adjustable shower control.)

Many more dwellings lacked hot water, and a 1940s resident of working-class Stanley Avenue in Yonkers, New York City, Jack Treacy, recalls (in an article for the *Yonkers History* website) that children in the apartments where he grew up used to wash at the kitchen sink, close to the coal stove on which water was boiled. Young Jack and his friends took a hot shower once a week, at the public bathhouse on nearby Jefferson Street.

Spartan conditions like these made the facilities in new housing developments such as Levittown seem like the last word in luxury. The original 1947 Levitt Cape Cods featured a single eight-by-five-foot bathroom with fluorescent lighting, a toilet and washbasin, and a tub with a shower fitting controlled by a "diverter"-type spout. Hot water was supplied from the same oil-fired boiler that provided the house's central heating, and up to eighteen gallons could be drawn over a five- to six-minute period—more than adequate for a shower, though a little ungenerous for a typical, thirty-gallon bath.

Later Levitt properties could accommodate a second attic bathroom, and by the end of the decade, some more upmarket homes had already been fitted with additional tubs and toilets, though the notion of providing a bath or shower for each bedroom in the house did not take hold until many years afterward.

The Bedroom

Many 1940s bedrooms offered their occupants a level of comfort that earlier generations would have marveled at. Residents of homes in Levittown, where the central heating was designed to maintain a steady seventy degrees, never had to tolerate cold of the kind described in *Main Street* by Sinclair Lewis, whose characters, the Kennicotts, needed to break the ice on their bedside washstand during the Minnesota winters. Beds themselves were reaching new heights of sophistication; products like the 1949 Burton Slumberon mattress, with its "exclusive Ortho-Flex innerspring construction," were a far cry from the primitive army cot used by the teenage James Thurber in the 1910s. (Thurber described the cot as "wide enough to sleep on comfortably only by putting up…the two sides which ordinarily hang down like the sideboards of a drop-leaf table"; the consequences of its dramatic collapse are immortalized in his classic short story *The Night The Bed Fell.*) And sufficiently wealthy and modish 1940s parents could model their children's bedrooms along the lines proposed by designer Raymond Loewy at the New York Metropolitan Museum's "Contemporary American

Right: An old-fashioned, plainly decorated bedroom in the rural New Mexico home of Juan Antonio Lopez— one of over a hundred shots taken of the Lopez household by Office of War Information photographer John Collier, Jr., who spent two days with them in early 1943.

Industrial Art" exhibition in 1940. Loewy's "Room for a five-year-old child" incorporated an elegant miniature bed, desk and dining table, a wall-mounted sketching board, and a soft, colorful carpet decorated with stars and planets.

Inevitably, such refinements were beyond the reach of poorer people. In January, 1943, photographer John Collier, Jr. visited Trampas, in northern New Mexico, to take pictures of the house and family of the town's mayor, Juan Antonio Lopez, which later formed part of the Office of War Information's *Portrait of America* collection. The Lopez dwelling is simple and functional, and the bedroom shown in one of Collier's shots, with its cheap but robust wooden and metal furnishings and floral wallpaper, looks similar to those in countless other rural homesteads. Inner cities often provided less agreeable lodgings. New Yorker Jack Treacy's Yonkers apartment included bedrooms with "no doors—you passed through one to the other," while the near-slum in Madison, Wisconsin, occupied by the family of struggling postwar student John R. Brochert (later a distinguished academic), had a bedroom floor "covered with torn carpet padding which was utterly filthy. […] The wallpaper was festooned from the walls, from which it had gradually separated and torn, [and] the furniture matched the general condition in which [the previous tenants] were leaving the place."

Brochert, like other Americans in similar circumstances, put up with his derelict apartment until, as he explained in his memoirs, he and his

Above: A 1940s teenager, relaxing in the privacy of her bedroom, takes the opportunity to catch up on some personal phone calls. She also has her own bedside radio (just visible on the nightstand).

aspirations by using a string of celebrities to promote bedroom furnishings. The Simmons company of Kenosha, Wisconsin, makers of Beautyrest mattresses, boasted an especially impressive roster of star names. In the 1920s and 1930s, Eleanor Roosevelt, Thomas Edison, H.G. Wells, and Henry Ford (among numerous others) had endorsed its products, and the postwar years saw prominent Beautyrest newspaper campaigns featuring Maureen O'Hara and Dorothy Lamour ("in sixty seconds, Dorothy learns how to buy a better mattress..."). Soon, though, the new medium of television would be demonstrating an even greater retailing power. Among its groundbreaking achievements during the early 1950s was the sale of over a million *I Love Lucy* bedroom sets, marketed in association with the show's producers, in only ninety days.

wife were able to "settle down with a permanent job somewhere and become homeowners." Families making such a move often found it practical and cost-effective to furnish their newly acquired property from scratch, and many manufacturers offered "bedroom sets," comprising a bed, dresser, mirror, chest, and vanity table, for little more than a hundred dollars. These items were frequently made from maple or pine, though moth-resistant red cedar was favored for the "hope chests" in which women kept the linen and clothing given to them before marriage to help them establish their new homes.

A three-piece suite, complemented by a couple of additional chairs and a nightstand, would have been very hard to accommodate in a standard twelve-by-twelve-foot Levittown master bedroom, although the Levitts provided a closet for extra storage, and other 1940s homes had larger rooms. But cramped conditions did not stop some householders from trying to re-create the luxurious interiors they saw in movies and magazines, and advertisers encouraged such

Above: A young woman adjusts her makeup at her bedroom vanity table as she dresses.

Left: A 1940s ad for a range of fitted sheets, available in a variety of attractive pastel shades.

VICTORY GARDENS
WILL HELP STRETCH YOUR POINT BUDGET!

CERTIFIED SEED POTATOES	"CAPITOL" LAWN SEED	10—6—4 FERTILIZER

The Garden and Yard

Large gardens were the preserve of country dwellers and a few privileged urbanites, but during the war years, Americans were encouraged to make their rations go further by using any available outdoor space—even a backyard or a window box—for cultivating vegetables. This "Victory Garden" scheme, modeled on the British "Dig For Victory" campaign, was launched in 1942, and proved immensely successful. More than 20 million plots were established, yielding an estimated million tons of produce per year, much of which was canned or bottled by prudent householders for consumption in the winter months.

Later in the decade, thanks to builders like the Levitts, many suburban dwellers acquired gardens of their own for the first time. Levittowners' new Cape Cods were provided with small, freshly seeded lawns, and a "Homeowners Guide," issued with each property, included strict instructions on how to tend them. The booklet explained the processes of rolling, watering, and fertilizing the growing grass, insisted that it should be mown weekly between April and November, and sternly reminded residents that "nothing makes a lawn—and a neighborhood— look shabbier than uncut grass and unsightly weeds. [Your lawn] will flourish if you take care of it—but it will quickly grow wild and unkempt if you don't." There were also restrictions on using Levittown yards for clothes drying: only revolving portable dryers were permitted, and women were asked not to leave laundry "hanging out on Sundays or holidays when you and your neighbors are most likely to be relaxing on your rear lawn."

Those 1940s householders without lawns could enjoy themselves in their yards or patios, where children were able to play safely, and families could gather for outdoor parties. Alfresco dining was perennially popular, and, after the lifting of wartime meat rationing, Americans were able to indulge in their favorite form of outdoor cooking, the barbecue—believed by many experts to be the oldest of all American cuisines, with its origins in the slow-grilling methods learned by fifteenth-century Spanish settlers from Arawak and Taino Indians!

Toys and Games

Below: The hot dogs are nearly ready at this mid-1940s barbecue, held in the pleasant surroundings of a suburban backyard. As usual, the man of the house is in charge of the cooking; his wife and their two guests look on expectantly, with drinks, dishes, and Heinz tomato ketchup at the ready!

Between 1942 and 1945, toys, games, and other playthings were often hard to obtain. Kids who dreamed of riding around on top-of-the-range bicycles like Schwinns and Iver-Johnsons sometimes had to make do with stripped-down "Victory" models. These resembled today's racing bikes, but were ridiculed by many 1940s children for their "skinny-tire" appearance. However, the toy business reaped occasional benefits from the war-related work that kept its products in such short supply. In 1943, scientist Richard James, who had been developing stabilizers for the delicate navigational instruments used in naval vessels, came up with the idea for Slinky—the famous steel spring capable of "walking downstairs." James marketed his invention soon after the war; it caught on quickly, and over 250 million have been sold worldwide since the mid-1940s.

The years of conflict helped to keep toy guns and model airplanes in steady demand—and inspired a few tasteless items like an "Atomic Bomb" puzzle, produced in 1945, in which jumping beans had to be guided into holes labeled "Hiroshima" and "Nagasaki." But long-standing favorites such as train sets still retained their popularity. The brand leaders in this highly competitive field were Lionel, whose recent innovations included "operating boxcars" that could unload their "cargoes" at the flick of a switch, and arch-rivals American Flyer, who launched their new "S"-gauge tracks in the mid-1940s.

The decade was also a golden era for board games. In 1949, Parker Brothers, the originators of Monopoly, licensed Cluedo, devised by Englishman Anthony Pratt and his wife during the war, from its British makers, Waddingtons. Renamed Clue for the U.S. market, it immediately became a best-seller. The previous year, Scrabble had made its debut. This classic word game evolved from two unsuccessful 1930s predecessors, Lexico and Criss-Crosswords, created by Alfred Mosher Butts, an architect from Poughkeepsie, New York. Scrabble itself was developed and initially manufactured by a Criss-Crosswords fan, James Brunot, who continued to produce it at a loss until sales finally took off in the early 1950s.

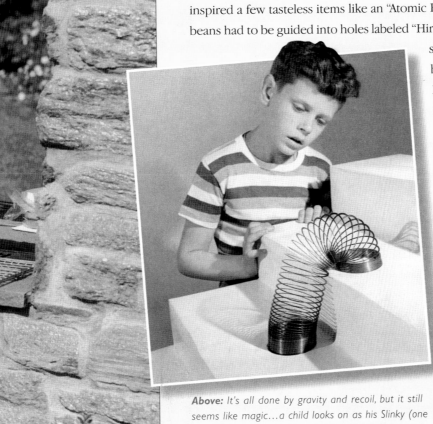

Above: It's all done by gravity and recoil, but it still seems like magic...a child looks on as his Slinky (one of the top-selling 1940s toys) "walks" downstairs.

Top right: An ad for Lionel, "the giant of the rails," whose train sets featured a range of exciting features to delight kids (and their dads!)—including built-in whistles, smoke generators, and "magne-traction."

Chicago's Union Stockyards, seen just before the outbreak of World War II.

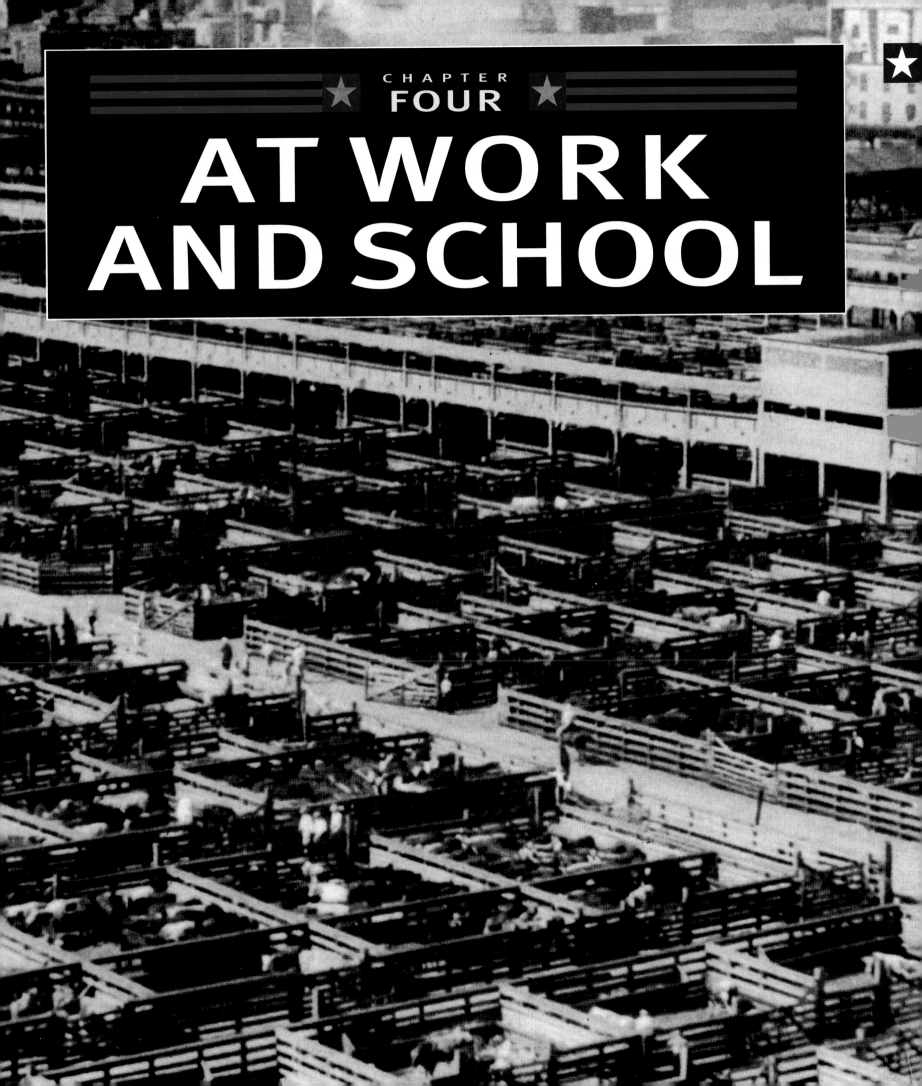

AT WORK
AND SCHOOL

Employment

Legislation and Postwar Industry

"This Congress hereby declares that it is the continuing policy and responsibility of the federal government...to coordinate and utilize all its plans, functions, and resources for the purpose of creating and maintaining, in a manner calculated to foster and promote free competitive enterprise and the general welfare, conditions under which there will be afforded useful employment opportunities, including self-employment, for those able, willing, and seeking to work, and to promote maximum employment, production, and purchasing power."

U.S. EMPLOYMENT ACT, 1946

Far right: *Coal cars lie empty at the National Coal Company's mine in Sygan, Pennsylvania during November, 1946, as the result of the strike instigated a month earlier by John L. Lewis, leader of the United Mine Workers Union.*

The unlovely prose of the 1946 Employment Act was cobbled together after lengthy disagreements, discussions, and compromises between the President and Congress. The more radical legislation originally put forward by Truman (including a commitment to full employment) had been brusquely rejected by his Republican opponents, and the eventual Act undertook to provide only "useful" and "maximum" job opportunities. It introduced other measures that increased government responsibility for workers' economic welfare, but was ultimately, in the words of historian James T. Patterson, "a far more cautious and non-committal step than many reformers had hoped for."

The Act became law at a time of unprecedented industrial strife. The lifting of wartime wage controls unleashed widespread pay demands, as well as calls by some of America's 18 million unionized employees for shorter working hours with no drop in salary. In fall, 1945, oil workers went on strike to try and obtain what their banners and slogans termed "52 for 40" (a return to their prewar 40-hour week for the same wages they had received for 52 hours' wartime labor). There was a walkout at General Motors that December, and action by steelmen, power workers, railroad employees, and others throughout 1946. Truman was obliged to intervene directly in several of these disputes, using the Navy to break the oil strike, brokering pay settlements in the steel and railroad industries, and briefly assuming control of the nation's coal mines during summer, 1946 in an attempt to avert a lengthy stoppage there. Negotiations with the highly influential United Mine Workers' Union

1940s TIMELINE

1940
Over 70 percent of all American 13–17 year-olds now attend high school; 50 percent graduate from it.

1943
Development of ENIAC (Electronic Numerical Integrator and Computer) begins at the University of Pennsylvania, funded by the U.S. Army. Work on the device is completed in 1946.

1945
36 percent of American women are in paid employment.

1946
116 million working hours are lost this year through strikes affecting mines, oil refineries, steel production, and other industries.

1947
Labor-Management Relations Act (Taft-Hartley Labor Act) is vetoed by President Truman but passed by Congress.

1950
Unemployment rises to 5.9 percent; 29 percent of women are now working.

boss, John L. Lewis, dragged on for the rest of the year, and led to Lewis being convicted for contempt after he defied Truman by calling a miners' strike that October.

Despite Truman's undoubted anger over this wave of militancy, he was hostile to the harsh measures against the unions that were soon to be brought before Congress. A new Bill, sponsored by two Republicans, Robert Taft and Fred Hartley, proposed the outlawing of "closed shops" (workplaces where all employees had to be union members), sought to give government the power to impose an eighty-day "cooling-off" period before strikes could be called, and threatened to restrict or ban many other areas of union activity. The legislation, formally titled the Labor-Management Relations Bill, but widely known as the Taft-Hartley Bill,

received strong support in the House and the Senate. Truman condemned it as discriminatory and vetoed it on June 20, 1947. It was, however, passed by Congress three days later.

Prolonged and costly union opposition to Taft-Hartley (the American Federation of Labor spent almost a million dollars lobbying against it) proved fruitless, and the Act led to a new, more pragmatic brand of industrial relations. Organized labor retained some of its previous power to gain benefits for its members, but, as Tom Kemp puts it in his study of the twentieth century U.S. economy, *The Climax of Capitalism*, employers began seeking "a quid pro quo" from their workers: "While ready to make wage concessions in the expansive years, [companies now] wanted a promise of industrial peace on the basis of long-term contracts and the maintenance of management prerogatives."

Below left: An affable settlement to a twenty-five-day-old strike by the United Auto Workers Union at Ford's Detroit plant in May, 1949, as the firm's Director of Industrial Relations, John Bugas (left), shakes hands with U.A.W. President, Walter P. Reuther. The walkout had been sparked by Ford's moves to speed up production.

Below: Aline Hester, a worker at a New York City food store, demonstrates her disapproval of the strike action being taken by her more militant colleagues (who had support from the American Federation of Labor) in November, 1946.

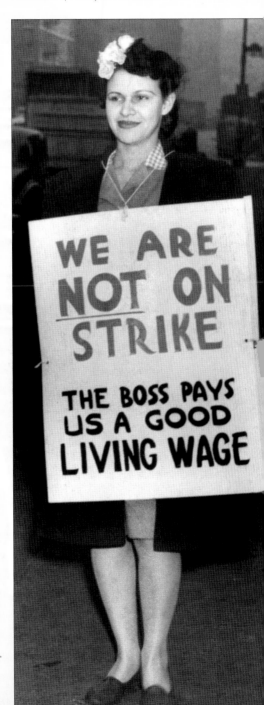

Farm Life

In the 1940s, technological progress was beginning to transform many areas of American enterprise. It affected rural areas and farms as well as cities and factories; the largest and most successful farms were now heavily mechanized, and their managers—the forerunners of today's "agribusinessmen"—were increasingly reliant on scientific developments as well as the latest tractors and combines. Artificial insemination enabled them to reduce costs and improve the quality of their livestock; new chemicals were available to remedy diseases, like citrus canker and Texas cattle fever, that had once wreaked havoc on their plants and animals; and their crop yields were boosted by a wide range of synthetic fertilizers and pesticides—a few of which, like DDT, would later prove to have unforeseen side-effects.

The image of the farmer himself was changing, too, thanks to the emergence of a new breed of agricultural tycoon with wealth and power equal to that of any urban entrepreneur. *Inside U.S.A.* by John Gunther includes a profile of Thomas C. Campbell, "the greatest wheat farmer in the world," who had built up his 95,000 acres of arable land in Montana with the help of a 2-million-dollar loan from financier J.P. Morgan. Campbell's methods of mass cultivation were highly effective, though controversial; critics accused him of damaging the soil through excessive planting, and described his managerial policies as "antisocial." Enjoying an international reputation, he had even traveled to Moscow in the 1920s to advise Josef Stalin and his ministers on farm mechanization.

Giants such as Campbell represented the future of profitable farming; those without large acreages or modern machinery often struggled to survive. From 1948 to 1952, Evelyn Birkby and her husband, Bob, rented a small farm in southwest Iowa, keeping it going by what she described in a 1994 interview with *Midwest Today* as "constant...hard, physical labor." The Birkbys stacked hay bales by hand in hundred-degree temperatures ("perspiration ran over our bodies, and the prickly bits of hay drifted down our shirts, into our socks, and around our waists"), braved sickness, accidents, and falling prices, and sometimes saw their precious crops destroyed by wind, rain, or drought. Evelyn went on to become a successful writer and broadcaster. She recalls many good times on the farm, but concedes that her "memories of simple, happy events and celebrations" are tempered by the harsh difficulties she endured.

Conditions like those experienced by the Birkbys drove millions of farm owners and tenants from the land throughout the 1940s. Other agricultural workers, including some of the poorest laborers and sharecroppers, had begun to lose their

JOHN DEERE GENERAL–PURPOSE
Tractors
New "A" and "B" Series

Above: The John Deere company was named for its founder, a blacksmith from Vermont who developed the first-ever steel plow in 1837, subsequently opening a factory at Moline, Illinois (still the firm's world headquarters) to produce his design. In 1918, Deere & Company began making motorized tractors, and went on to become a leading manufacturer of all kinds of agricultural equipment. By the 1940s, it was a multi-million dollar business.

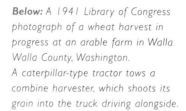

Left: A number of farmers in California and elsewhere hired illegal immigrants to toil in their fields for low wages. This photograph, taken by Harry Pennington in 1948, shows two Mexicans tying mustard greens into bunches—an arduous task made harder by the scorching summer sun.

Below: A 1941 Library of Congress photograph of a wheat harvest in progress at an arable farm in Walla Walla County, Washington. A caterpillar-type tractor tows a combine harvester, which shoots its grain into the truck driving alongside.

Above: 1940s migrant workers were often housed in makeshift accommodation of the sort seen here. Individual "homes," including trailers and canvas-roofed shacks, are laid out around a larger building providing communal facilities for laundry and other basic needs.

livelihoods and homes in the Depression years, when migrant camps, similar to those described in John Steinbeck's famous 1939 novel *The Grapes of Wrath,* were set up to feed and shelter them. During the war, these camps—many of which moved, with their residents, from location to location—were used to channel workers into areas where farm labor was in short supply. In 1942, the U.S. government secured a new source of temporary manpower, signing a agreement permitting thousands of Mexican *braceros* to undertake agricultural work on the American side of the border. Over the following decades, they were to become a mainstay of American farming, especially in the Western states.

Left: Full steam ahead—a recently recruited group of women railroad mechanics smile enthusiastically as they start their shift at a New York City marshalling yard in February, 1942.

Women at Work

Women were a vital and highly visible part of the wartime workforce. However, their motivation for taking their jobs was often portrayed—at least, by contemporary, generally male journalists and copywriters—as purely patriotic and, perhaps, romantic. One 1943 Texaco ad shows a young woman, Alice, wielding a drill in an airplane factory. As she works, she thinks of her fiancé, Eddie (now with his squadron), remembers their conversation about "the home they would some day have together," and reflects that "they'd have it now if it wasn't for Adolf." The ad's punchline, *"Alice and Eddie know why they're fighting,"* implies that once Hitler is defeated and Eddie comes home, Alice will have no further need to stay in employment—and after the war, millions of Alices did indeed down their tools and returned to a life of domesticity.

Other women had broader horizons. In the past, female college graduates had often been steered into teaching or the handful of alternative jobs, such as secretarial and clerical positions, regarded as "acceptable" for their sex. But during the war, a wider range of career opportunities opened up, especially in science and technology. Women made key contributions to defense work, including the Manhattan Project and the development of the ENIAC computer at the University of Pennsylvania. In 1943, airplane manufacturer Curtiss-Wright launched a ten-month "Cadette" program for female engineering students, some of whom later became important figures in aviation—a field in which women had previously taken only subsidiary roles.

After the war, though, the return of large numbers of men from military service made it more difficult for women—even if they had impressive academic qualifications—to find jobs suited to their abilities. Historian Cynthia Harrison observes that, with males resuming their former domination of industry, and females going back to more traditional "women's work," "Rosie the Riveter had become a file clerk." There was also a legal problem: as Elinore M. Herrick pointed out in a 1943 *New York Times Magazine* article, the Selective Service Act "made it mandatory for employers to reemploy returning soldier[s] if there

Above: This in-store display, seen at Lansburgh's in Washington, D.C. in May, 1943, uses a uniform-clad mannequin, combined with posters supplied by the U.S. Office of War Information, as part of a nationwide campaign to encourage women to enroll as student nurses. Later nursing recruitment drives featured an illustration of a wounded soldier on a stretcher, and a stark slogan: "Urgent! You Must Help!"

[was] any job at all for [them], ejecting the employee hired since the soldier left." Those employees were frequently women, whose prospects for longer-term postwar careers were damaged both by this well-intentioned legislation and by other, more openly discriminatory practices. Although the female workforce numbered some 18 million by 1950, they remained ineligible for many jobs, especially more senior positions, and, until the passage of the Equal Pay Act in 1963, usually received substantially lower salaries than their male colleagues.

At School

Children throughout the U.S.A. shared a similar routine at the start of each school day during the 1940s: an 8 o'clock assembly at which they said prayers, sang songs and hymns, pledged allegiance to the American flag, and received a short address from their principal or schools superintendent. However, most other aspects of their education—what they studied, the resources they had access to, and even their teachers' salaries—were subject to considerable variation.

This was partly due to local conditions. While schools received some federal funding, a large proportion of their revenue was raised at state or county level, and pupils and teachers in the poorest areas were inevitably disadvantaged as a result. John Gunther's *Inside U.S.A.* contains a grim description of a school for black children in Georgia, run by an underpaid staff of four, and housed "at the end of a red-yellow unpaved road full of mud and rocks…in a shaky warped frame building" with no library, playground, science lab, adequate heating, or even indoor toilets. Wealthier communities could afford far better premises; their schools were often the biggest, most impressive properties in town, with modern, well-equipped facilities that were frequently used by local adults as well as students.

What children learned in the classroom itself was determined by their performance in the aptitude tests they took as fourth-graders. Those with the highest scores followed a "College Preparatory" curriculum that included math, English, science, history, Latin and modern languages, although, until the advent of the GI Bill (see pages 22–23), comparatively few pupils were actually able to go on to higher education. The remaining students joined the "General" school program; this combined tuition in math, languages, and other basics with a grounding in practical skills such as woodworking and mechanical drawing (for boys) and cooking and sewing (for girls). Kids were also separated by gender for daily gym sessions and, in some states, weekly sex education classes.

Dress codes and other rules—though these, too, differed slightly from school to school—were strictly enforced. Sneakers, dungarees, and later, jeans, were usually forbidden; pupils showing up in them could expect to be sent home (if it was within walking distance) to change, and then penalized for their resultant "illegal" absence from class. Smoking was an expellable offense (teachers were also generally forbidden from indulging on school premises, and sometimes even within sight of the school), and eating in class was also a punishable transgression. Punctuality and overall conduct, as well as academic work, were assessed and graded on twice-yearly report cards. High standards of courtesy and diligence were encouraged, and columnists and pamphleteers like M. Thelma McAndless, author of the oppressively titled *Manners Today* (1943), were always ready to lecture teenagers on the evils of laziness, truancy, and "cribbing" at school ("Have you been regular in attendance? Is it your policy to blunder into class a few minutes late? Do you then slap books, rattle papers, and annoy your seat mate? Do you copy his work? Don't fib. What kind of school citizen are you?") But students could escape the pressures of the classroom on the sports field. Football and basketball were especially popular, though soccer was starting to gain acceptance in some areas, and school teams often enjoyed an enthusiastic following within their local communities.

Photographs on these pages: *First graders at elementary school in Tomball, TX, recite the pledge of allegiance (right); a girls' gym class at Caroline County High School, VA, in 1949 (top left); senior pupils in the same school's chemistry lab (above).*

In the Office

The typical 1940s office was, in many ways, a formal, hierarchical set-up, in which men and women dressed soberly, put in long hours, and knew their place. Bosses and more senior employees worked behind closed doors with their secretaries and assistants, while central pools of junior staff, almost invariably female, undertook clerical and copy-typing tasks, seated at rows of manual typewriters.

Above: A smartly suited mid-1940s American executive refreshes himself with a glass of water from the cooler in his office. The rigidities of contemporary etiquette probably prevent him from making himself more comfortable by removing his jacket!

The gulf between the typing pool and the inner sanctums of management was formidable, though bosses were always expected to show subordinates what Emily Post, whose *Etiquette*, published in 1922, still stood as Holy Writ in many quarters of American society, described as "courteous consideration." However, Miss Post was careful to warn "superior officers" not to come across as "mincing,

foppish, or effeminate," and to remind them that any lapses of decorum or displays of "ill-breeding" might offend clients as well as colleagues. "If you…entered a man's office and found him lolling back in a tipped swivel chair, his feet above his head, [and] the ubiquitous cigar in his mouth…you would be impressed not so much by his lack of good manners as by his bad business policy, because of the incompetence that his attitude suggests."

Working relations between executives and their personal secretaries did not always adhere to Post's strict precepts. As Harvard Business School Professor Rosabeth Moss Kanter's *Men and Women of the Corporation* (1977) explains, a male boss would often treat his female assistant in a "patrimonial" way, "mak[ing] demands at [his] own discretion and arbitrarily; choos[ing] secretaries on grounds that enhance[d] [his] own personal status rather than meeting organizational efficiency tests; [and] expect[ing] personal service with limits negotiated privately." Those limits could stretch well beyond work-related matters, with P.A.s sometimes being asked to make social arrangements for employers, and even paying domestic bills on their behalf. Secretaries themselves rarely received large salaries—managers frequently rewarded them with, in Kanter's phrase, "roses rather than raises"—though their inside knowledge, and their skill at controlling access to their bosses, could ensure them a substantial degree of status and influence in the companies they served.

Office Tools

Most 1940s office equipment was based on long-established, highly familiar technology. New products were gradually starting to appear, but many of these—including the electric typewriter, launched by Remington in the mid-1920s—were still comparative rarities, unlike the mechanically operated adding machines being made in their millions by Burroughs and other firms, or the rotary card index (later known as a Rolodex) invented before the Depression by former Yale mathematics professor, Irving Fisher.

For their office printing needs, clerks and typists generally relied on stencil duplicators like Mimeographs. These used a process in which a wax-coated "skin" was cut with a typewriter or stylus, mounted on an ink-filled drum, and rolled onto successive sheets of paper. File copies of letters and other documents were made with carbon paper; the first-ever photocopier, invented by Chester Carlson, appeared in the late 1940s, but it was to be over a decade before Xerox introduced a machine fast and practical enough for commercial purposes.

Business telecommunications were a mixture of ancient and modern. Phones were mostly used for local calls; it was often cheaper to send Western Union telegrams to offices and clients in more distant cities. However, teletype, which allowed operators to transmit messages between machines linked by telegraph, had been commonplace since the previous century, and the more recent Telex system (especially convenient for overseas communications) was being adopted by some firms.

Other important technologies lay just around the corner. Magnetic tape, developed by Germany during the war years, was soon to replace wire as the recording medium for office dictating machines. In the mid-1950s, a Texan typist, Bette Nesmith Graham (mother of future Monkee Michael Nesmith) would use her kitchen food mixer to make the first batch of what was later marketed as Liquid Paper. Before long, the adoption of mainframe computers by a few large firms would herald a far more significant and far-reaching event—the start of the digital revolution.

A Decade of Innovation

The 1940s saw the emergence of a host of new technologies and inventions, some of them created by companies whose managerial style was almost as revolutionary as their products. One of the first "hi-tech" startups in the area of northern California later known as "Silicon Valley," Hewlett-Packard, began as a two-man operation in 1939 but grew rapidly over the next decade. The firm made its initial reputation with an audio oscillator used by Walt Disney on the soundtrack of *Fantasia*, and went on to manufacture a variety of signal generators and microwave devices before moving into computers during the 1960s. Its founders, Bill Hewlett and Dave Packard, believed in "management by walking around." Their offices had no doors, allowing bosses to mingle freely with their employees, with whom they were on first-name terms, and to discuss ideas and problems in a relaxed, informal atmosphere. This agreeable approach—very different from the stiff formality of most 1940s workplaces—proved to be good for business, and was subsequently adopted by several of Hewlett-Packard's rivals, who also followed the company's lead in providing health insurance and stock options for its staff.

Among other comparatively small firms with big ideas was Thermo King of Minneapolis, which introduced the first reliable system of food refrigeration for trucks. Founded in the late 1930s, it quickly developed a range of lightweight, powerful mobile cooling units—including models whose temperature could be adjusted to suit a wide range of cargoes, from fresh vegetables to ice cream.

Left and opposite page above left:
The thirty-ton ENIAC (an acronym for "Electronic Numerical Integrator and Computer") was developed at the University of Pennsylvania during the war years, and used to perform critical calculations for the Manhattan Project and other key defense operations.

Right: A Fender Telecaster. Leo Fender's first great guitar design took shape during the late 1940s, and went into production in 1950, though it was not given its final name until the following year.

Thermo King's near contemporary, Polaroid, set up by a Harvard dropout, Edwin Herbert Land, spent the war years producing specialized target finding gear and other optical devices for the military, before launching its legendary instant camera in 1948. It caught on quickly, and was later featured in a series of memorable TV ads, demonstrating the entire Polaroid process—from pressing the shutter to unpeeling the finished photo—in a single, sixty-second spot.

At around the same time, former radio repairman Clarence Leo Fender was establishing his fledgling guitar and amplifier manufacturing business in Fullerton, California, near Los Angeles. Already highly respected as an instrument builder, Leo was shortly to start work on an innovative solid-body guitar—known initially as the "Electric Standard" and the "Broadcaster" before being rechristened "Telecaster"—that would make him internationally famous, and inspire millions of budding musicians to take up the instrument. Fender subsequently created several more classic electric models, such as the

Stratocaster (favored by Buddy Holly and Jimi Hendrix), the Jazzmaster and the Jaguar, as well as the first-ever electric bass guitar, the Precision. All are still being made and played today.

Larger corporations were also at the forefront of some of the most significant manufacturing and scientific breakthroughs of the 1940s. Perhaps the very greatest of these was the invention of the transistor in 1947 by three scientists from Bell Laboratories (the research wing of AT&T), William Shockley, John Bardeen, and Walter Brattain. Prior to their achievements, all electronic devices, including early computers like ENIAC, had relied on vacuum tubes, which were bulky, ran hot, and had a high failure rate. As Paul Freiberger and Michael Swaine's history of the computer, *Fire In The Valley*, explains, solid-state transistors "did everything the vacuum tube did, and did it better." They could also be combined into integrated circuits, later known as silicon chips, which were soon to be the building blocks for a new generation of compact, versatile electronics. It was Shockley, Bardeen, and Brattain who effectively put the silicon in Silicon Valley; their invention was patented in 1950, and six years later the three men were awarded the Nobel Prize for their groundbreaking contribution to physics.

... relays the results of ... al election to voters.

THAT'S ENTERTAINMENT

The Development of American
Radio and TV

Frasier: People of Dad's generation would sit around the radio each night, absolutely mesmerized.

Martin: We were a simple people. It was the little orange glow that got us.

Frasier: I happen to think radio drama was marvelous. People actually had to use their imagination. Then TV came along and ruined it.

Martin: Yeah, and it scared us, too. We kept wondering how all those little people got trapped in that box. FROM FRASIER, "HAM RADIO" EPISODE, 1996

Commercial radio in America is generally accepted to have begun on August 20, 1920, when station WWJ made its first transmission, featuring a recorded music program, from a studio in downtown Detroit. WWJ was operated by a local newspaper, the *Detroit News*, and had obtained its license to broadcast from the Department of the Navy. However, another radio pioneer, KDKA, based in Wilkinsburg, Pennsylvania, and serving the Pittsburgh area, acquired its authorization and callsign from the Department of Commerce just three months later, and is one of several other contenders for the title of the nation's longest-established continuously operating station.

Initially, these broadcasters served only small, localized audiences; fewer than 10,000 wireless sets were in use at the start of the 1920s, and low transmitter power made long-distance reception impossible. Soon, though, public demand grew, and technicians began

Above: The first U.S. TV star? "Felix the Cat" appears in a 1930s test transmission.

to devise methods of extending the geographical reach of their audio signals. The introduction of so-called "chain broadcasting," enabling stations to be linked up via landlines, led to the setting-up of the first permanent radio network, NBC (National Broadcasting Company). By 1927, its owners, RCA, General Electric, and Westinghouse, were running two separate ("red" and "blue") networks, and a rival group of interconnected affiliates, the Columbia Broadcasting System (CBS), had also been launched. In 1934, some of the (mostly smaller) stations that had remained independent of NBC and CBS came together to form a cooperatively run network of their own, the Mutual Broadcasting System (MBS). The American Broadcasting Company (ABC) took over NBC's "blue" network in 1945.

These developments set the scene for radio's "Golden Era." Throughout the 1930s and '40s, its schedules were studded with star

Above: *Teatime in front of the TV in about 1950. On the screen are George Burns and Gracie Allen, then starring in their own top-rated CBS comedy show.*

Above: *This Belmont shirt-pocket radio, introduced soon after the war, was the first portable set of its kind. It was ingeniously designed, with an earphone cable that doubled as an antenna.*

names from variety, drama, and music, often appearing alongside younger performers who were making their own reputations (and fortunes) on the airwaves. The networks could afford to pay their artists handsomely, thanks to a steady rise in advertising revenues and listener numbers; by the mid-1930s, over 60 percent of all American homes and a million and a half automobiles were equipped with radios. The medium was also becoming an implicitly trusted source of news and information as well as entertainment. Record audiences of 90 million tuned in to FDR's declaration of war in December, 1941, and reports by foreign correspondents such as Edward R. Murrow brought home the realities of global conflict more powerfully and movingly than almost any printed word.

Meanwhile, television was getting off to a slower start. Early transmissions, including the images of the cartoon character "Felix the Cat" first broadcast by RCA in 1929, had relied on low-definition (less than 120-line) mechanical scanning. This was eventually replaced by a superior electronic system, and in 1939, a regular TV service began in some areas, although public interest seemed limited, and there was little protest when most television broadcasts were suspended for the duration of the war. But the medium's fortunes were about to change dramatically, as we shall see later in this chapter. By the late 1940s, TV's advertising revenues were approaching radio's total earning power, and a massive subsequent rise in set ownership—over half the nation's households had TVs by 1954—would soon mark the end of radio's long decades of media dominance.

1940s TIMELINE

1939
The National Broadcasting Company gives a public TV demonstration at the New York World's Fair. By the end of the year, both NBC and the Columbia Broadcasting System (CBS) are transmitting several hours of television a week.

1940
A third television network is set up by the DuMont Company.

1941
On July 1, the Bulova watch company sponsors the first-ever TV commercial on New York City's WNBT-TV in New York City.

At the outbreak of war in December, there are twenty U.S. TV stations, although technical limitations largely confine reception to the Eastern seaboard. During the war years, most of these stations are forced to close down.

1945
Numbers of TV stations and hours of transmissions begin to increase rapidly. However, at this stage, only about 7,000 homes have sets.

January, 1947
Harry S. Truman becomes the first President to broadcast his State of the Union address on television.

June 20, 1948
Ed Sullivan hosts the first edition of his Sunday night CBS variety show *The Toast of the Town*, with guests including Richard Rodgers, Oscar Hammerstein II, and Dean Martin. The program quickly establishes itself as a favorite with TV audiences. It is renamed for its presenter in 1955, and runs until 1971.

1950
TV ownership has risen to 3,880,000— approximately 9 percent of American homes now have sets.

Classic Radio Comedy

Charles Correll and Freeman Gosden were two white writer/performers with roots in vaudeville. In 1926, they launched a comedy series on Chicago's station WGN in which they portrayed a pair of Negroes from the Deep South, Sam and Henry, who have come to the Windy City to make new lives for themselves. Two years later, the characters, renamed Amos and Andy for contractual reasons, got their own six-day-a-week, fifteen-minute show on a rival Chicago station, WMAQ. This program, subsequently networked by NBC, continued until 1943, when it switched to a weekly half-hour format that remained in the schedules for another twelve years. In 1951, *Amos 'n' Andy* made the transition onto TV, and the duo's three decades of stardom has earned them a place in the history books as one of the best-loved comedy acts of all time.

Amos 'n' Andy broke new ground in many areas. It was the first radio serial to use regular characters, the first to be broadcast twice (enabling West Coast audiences to hear it at a more convenient time), and the first to rely almost entirely on just two actors—during the program's early years, Correll and Gosden played not only Amos and Andy but virtually all the supporting characters as well. It also stirred some controversy: several prominent newspapers accused it of exploiting and stereotyping African-Americans, though other commentators rallied to the show's support, and it was, in its day, widely enjoyed by black listeners.

Chicago also gave network radio *Fibber McGee and Molly*, a sitcom with a record of on-air achievement second only to that of *Amos 'n' Andy*. It starred husband-and-wife team Jim and Marian Jordan, and was broadcast on NBC from 1935 to 1959. Itself a by-product of an earlier show, *Smackout*, *Fibber McGee* went on to spawn a popular spin-off, *The Great Gildersleeve*, first broadcast in 1941. The braggadocious Fibber, the kindly, sensible Molly, and the bumbling Gildersleeve were perennial radio favorites, although attempts to transfer them to TV proved unsuccessful. Sadly, the Jordans' professional partnership ended in 1960, when Marian was diagnosed with cancer; she died a year later.

As well as comedy dramas like those mentioned above, radio showcased numerous variety and stand-up series. Jack Benny, Red Skelton, and Bob Hope were among the major stars nurtured by the medium, while Abbott and Costello got their first big break when they guested on a program fronted by singer Kate Smith in 1938. Other

Right: Charles Correll (left) and Freeman Gosden, in "blackface" make-up for the early '50s TV version of their famous series Amos 'n' Andy, which they wrote and starred in together. Correll and Gosden started out as musical entertainers, and developed their gift for comedy after establishing themselves on radio in Chicago.

Below: Edgar Bergen demonstrates his muscle-power to a monocled Charlie McCarthy in a nautically flavored sketch from one of their 1940s shows.

Below: Bud Abbott and Lou Costello performing one of their classic comedy routines on NBC radio in the mid-1940s.

radio success stories have a touch of the bizarre about them. Ventriloquist Edgar Bergen and his dummy Charlie McCarthy built up a huge following on NBC and CBS in the 1940s, but it was only after Bergen moved to TV that audiences were truly able to appreciate his voice-throwing skills!

Big-name comedy and variety was an expensive and often risky undertaking, and it is significant that nearly all the major 1940s shows in this genre were made by the "big two" networks. However, the less wealthy Mutual Broadcasting System managed to introduce one important name to the airwaves: Henry Morgan, whose *Here's Morgan*, described by radio historian Elizabeth McLeod as "a fifteen-minute stream-of-consciousness monologue," ran on MBS until 1943. After war service, Morgan attained wider fame as a movie actor, and he later became a long-time panellist on CBS-TV's *I've Got A Secret*.

Below: A quartet of top comedians—Milton Berle, Jack Benny, Bob Hope, and Red Skelton—clowning for the camera as they arrive at Los Angeles' Shrine Auditorium in March, 1942. All four had already triumphed in radio, and were soon to enjoy further success in television, while Hope's appearances in the Road to… movies with Bing Crosby and Dorothy Lamour were also bringing him a taste of Hollywood stardom.

Music on Radio

Music of all kinds, frequently performed live, was a vital ingredient of 1940s radio. Most variety and comedy shows had their own resident groups and featured soloists; whole series, such as Kay Kyser's *Kollege of Musical Knowledge*, were built around popular ensembles and bandleaders; and the networks carried regular evening relays of major jazz and swing concerts. The technical quality of these remote broadcasts was sometimes less than ideal. According to George T. Simon's book, *The Big Bands*, "CBS and NBC sent an announcer and an engineer to each [event], but Mutual, a less wealthy network, had one man perform both functions. This required both a good ear and a good voice. Unfortunately very few men had both." However, audiences and musicians loved the immediacy and excitement of the shows, which often attracted lucrative sponsorship.

Classical music was also an important part of the networks' output. In 1937, NBC formed its own symphony orchestra, with Arturo Toscanini as principal conductor. It remained in existence until 1954, giving thousands of live and studio performances under him and other leading maestri such as Leopold Stokowski and Pierre Monteux. CBS, too, was responsible for an impressive range of serious music broadcasts, and in 1939 it presented the first-ever program of opera on television—a specially staged studio performance of extracts from Leoncavallo's *I Pagliacci*.

So-called "platter shows," featuring disc jockeys and music from commercially released phonograph records, only accounted for a few hours' programming a week on most 1940s stations. The term "disc jockey" is thought to have been coined by presenter Martin Block, host of *Make Believe Ballroom* on New York's WNEW, in which he created the illusion of a live performance with a skilful combination of records, including a specially produced theme signature by Glenn Miller's band. Such formats displayed far greater subtlety and imagination than the scores of standardized, cheaply made DJ programs that pervaded the airwaves during the 1950s, as radio began losing its revenues to TV.

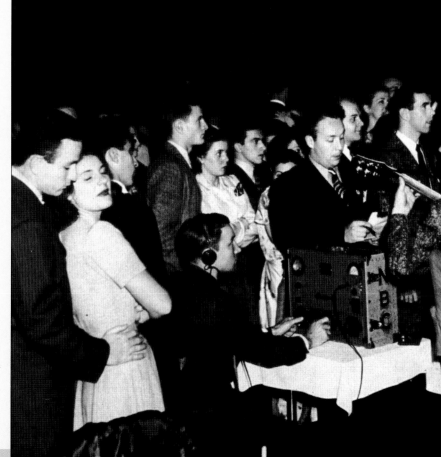

Basie and the Famous Door

Radio played a vital role in the careers of many leading jazz musicians, and for pianist and bandleader Bill Basie it brought not only valuable exposure but a new stage name. In the mid-1930s, he was working with his nine-piece band, the Barons of Rhythm, at the Reno Club in Kansas City. One evening, the announcer from station W9XBY, which was relaying the shows, decided that Basie deserved an "honorary" title like those used by Duke Ellington and King Oliver, and started referring to him on air as "Count"—a sobriquet that soon caught on with the musician's colleagues and fans!

Basie's appearances on W9XBY led to greater things. Within a few years, he had expanded his lineup and enjoyed his first major recording successes. In 1938, he and his orchestra began a residency at New York's Famous Door club, with network broadcast coverage by CBS. In his autobiography, *Good Morning Blues*, Basie recalls that the relays from the Famous Door were "the very best thing that could happen for the band, because we had excellent airtime, and that was when radio was it. People used to tell us about how they would go out and drive through Central Park listening to us on their radios in their cars, and those jitney cab drivers out in Chicago used to run up and down South Parkway digging us on their radios, too. [...] With those broadcasts going out over a coast-to-coast hookup, we could finally really begin to feel that we were making it into the big time." The Basie band was to return regularly to the Famous Door until the outbreak of war in 1941.

Above: *Actress Jane Russell gets a music lesson from bandleader Kay (the "Ol' Professor") Kyser as they rehearse for a radio broadcast in the early 1940s.*

Opposite page far left: *The Andrews Sisters on the air for CBS with Glenn Miller in the early 1940s.*

Below: *Trumpeter Charlie Spivak (known to fans as "the sweetest horn in the world") leads his ensemble for a prewar concert date being broadcast live by NBC radio.*

Above: *The Count Basie Orchestra at New York's Famous Door club in 1938—the first year of their residency. With Basie (on piano) are bassist Walter Page, drummer Jo Jones (at the back), guitarist Freddie Green, and (standing) tenor saxophonist Herschel Evans.*

Radio Drama

1940s radio offered a range of drama for all tastes and ages, and among its most avid fans were the youngsters who would hurry home from school each day to catch up on the latest exploits of their fantasy heroes. These were usually presented in fifteen-minute episodes—half-hour children's shows began to be introduced toward the end of the decade—which were often artfully structured, with cliff-hanging conclusions that left their audiences clamoring for more—and tuning in tomorrow.

George W. Trendle, the manager of station WXYZ in Detroit, devised two of the best-loved and longest running kids' serials, *The Lone Ranger* and *The Green Hornet*. The Lone Ranger (with his Indian sidekick Tonto, and the Great Horse, Silver) emerged in January, 1933, and was soon the hottest property on the newly formed Mutual network. Despite frequent casting changes, and the death in a 1941 automobile accident of Earle Graser, who had played the Ranger for the previous eight years, the show continued on radio until September, 1954, and also became a TV favorite. The Green Hornet, another masked fighter for justice, was the Lone Ranger's grandnephew. He made his debut in 1936, and proved to be a successful and enduring character, though he never quite attained the legendary status of his older relative.

Several children's radio programs were adapted from cartoons and comics. *Terry and the Pirates*, created in strip form by artist Milton Caniff in 1934, made the transition to NBC three years later; and in February, 1940, two years after Superman had first appeared on America's newsstands, his exploits were serialized on Mutual, with Bud Collyer in the title role. Another series, *Tom Mix*, was based (albeit very loosely) on a real person—Thomas Hezekiah Mix (1880–1940), a former Oklahoma lawman, silent-movie star, and circus proprietor, whose fictionalized Western crimebusting adventures aired regularly from 1933 to 1950.

Left: *Lucille Ball gives a dramatic guest performance in* Dime a Dance, *an episode of CBS's popular weekly radio series,* Suspense. *The program, which was sponsored by Roma Wines, was broadcast on January 13, 1944; six months later, Ms. Ball appeared in a second* Suspense *show titled* The Ten Grand.

In the early evening, radio stations tended to schedule shows that could be enjoyed by the whole family. Adaptations of classic crime stories (as well as more melodramatic mysteries like the one affectionately parodied in Frasier's *Ham Radio*—see pages 78–79) were always popular,

as were serials like *The Shadow*, launched back in 1930, which had, for a while, starred Orson Welles as the mysterious hero with the memorable catchphrase "Who knows what evil lurks in the hearts of men?" The series' original sponsors, publishers Street and Smith, went on to issue a Shadow fiction magazine, as well as hundreds of pulp novels about the character. Much of this material, though not the Shadow scripts themselves, was written by the prolific Walter B. Gibson, who used the *nom de plume* Maxwell Grant. During the series' later years, The Shadow was played by Bret Morrison; it ran until 1954 and was subsequently adapted for TV.

Further thrills were provided by *I Love A Mystery*, featuring Jack Packard and his pals Doc Long and Reggie York—a feisty trio who end up running a Hollywood detective agency. The serial, launched in 1939 by NBC writer/producer Carlton E. Morse (who claimed it was inspired by Dumas' *The Three Musketeers*), eventually transferred to CBS, ABC, and Mutual, and Packard and his associates went on to appear in a number of low-budget movies. Morse was also responsible for a very different kind of radio classic—the epic *One Man's Family*, which he dedicated "to the mothers and fathers of the younger generation and to their bewildering offspring." This award-winning serial traced the lives and experiences of the Barbours, a fictional California family, and ran on NBC for a staggering twenty-seven years (1932–1959).

The networks also broadcast series of single plays, often with impressively starry casts. In the 1930s, Orson Welles' *Mercury Theater*

Left: The January 1, 1933 number of The Shadow Magazine. Launched two years earlier, this title survived until 1948, and some of the stories and artwork featured in it were later reissued. Its creators, New York-based publishers Street and Smith, also produced similar magazines featuring Doc Savage and other pulp favorites.

Above: Brace Beemer in costume as The Lone Ranger. Beemer, formerly the announcer on the Ranger's weekly Mutual Network radio show, took over the title role after the death of Earle Graser, and played it until 1954. His distinctive vocal delivery strongly influenced Clayton Moore, who became the TV Lone Ranger in 1949.

on the Air had terrified the nation with *The War of the Worlds,* and had also dramatized *Dracula, The Count of Monte Cristo*, and other favorites. However, the most glittering productions of the 1940s were undoubtedly the *Lux Radio Theater* shows made in Hollywood by CBS. These brought the very biggest box office names—such as Errol Flynn, Judy Garland, Laurence Olivier, and Katharine Hepburn—to the microphone, and until 1945, the programs were hosted by none other than Cecil B. DeMille. They were transmitted every Monday evening throughout the decade, and must have been the highlight of many a radio listener's week.

News and Sport on Radio

The earliest news event to receive radio coverage was the presidential election of 1920, whose results, culminating in the victory of Republican candidate Warren Harding, were carried live on Pennsylvania station KDKA (see pages 78–79). Current affairs broadcasting developed rapidly over the next few years. H.V. Kaltenborn, later a senior NBC journalist, claimed (during a Columbia University oral history interview) to have been "the first person to interpret news on the air" at New York's WEAF in 1923, and before long, other stations were carrying regular bulletins derived from wire service material.

This angered America's press barons, who often found themselves being "scooped" by the broadcasters, and waged a lengthy campaign (the so-called "Press-Radio War") to restrict the duration and number of news summaries. However, their efforts ultimately proved unsuccessful, and by the late 1930s, radio was a trusted current affairs medium, with its own skilled correspondents and commentators. Perhaps the most distinguished of them was Edward R. Murrow, who was appointed CBS's Head of Talks in 1935, at the age of only twenty-seven. In 1937, he became the network's European bureau chief, and the leader of a formidable team of journalists (the "Murrow Boys") which would soon be covering the events of World War II for CBS listeners back home.

Murrow's own wartime dispatches are justly famous (see pages 12–13—he reported from London and other key locations, including the concentration camp at Buchenwald following its liberation in 1945), and the work of his colleague, William L. Shirer (1904–1993), who was based in Berlin until 1941, also merits especial mention. After the war, Shirer left broadcasting (he went on to write a highly acclaimed history of the Third Reich), and Murrow briefly served as CBS's director of public affairs before returning to radio journalism and, later, appearing on television. Meanwhile, a wide range of home-based news broadcasters had established themselves on rival stations. H.V. Kaltenborn (see above) was

Left: CBS newsman Edward R. Murrow (left) interviews U.S. General Omar Bradley (1893–1981) in about 1945. Bradley, a key military commander during the European campaigns at the conclusion of World War II, was subsequently to become chairman of the Joint Chiefs of Staff, and (in 1950) General of the Army.

already an institution at NBC—his listeners included President Harry Truman, who apparently enjoyed mimicking Kaltenborn's distinctive accent and delivery—and, for those with a taste for gossip and controversy, Walter Winchell's weekly shows on the same network, and subsequently for ABC, were unmissable.

Like their counterparts in news, radio sports commentators grew markedly in sophistication during the 1940s. As Frank Buxton and Bill Owen observe in their book *1920 to 1950, The Big Broadcast*, non-specialist announcers had once been "assigned to describe sporting events as routinely as they might [have been] sent to cover a news story or...a band remote." Sometimes, they were even obliged to stay in the studio, basing their broadcasts on incoming wire reports without being able to see the action. Those days, though, were largely gone, and the finest 1940s sports presenters were mostly dedicated experts, adept at play-by-play description and analysis. Among the best known were Harry Wismer (for football on ABC), Red Barber (baseball, CBS), and Clem McCarthy (boxing and racing, NBC). There was, nevertheless, still room for hyperbole, idiosyncrasy, and occasional flights of fancy in their commentaries—one man particularly renowned for these was NBC's Bill Stern, who once declared to the nation that Abraham Lincoln's dying words had been "Save baseball"!

Below: Hollywood actresses Fanny Brice (left) and Judy Garland guesting on NBC's Maxwell House MGM Hour in the early 1940s. The show's $25,000 weekly budget enabled it to attract many other major stars.

Left: An immaculately dressed Bob Hope rehearsing for NBC's Colgate Comedy Hour. The program was launched in 1950; Eddie Cantor was its first presenter, and Hope began hosting it two years later.

Below: Soprano Lily Pons (left) is interviewed for NBC radio as part of the network's Texaco-sponsored coverage of live performances from New York's Metropolitan Opera.

And Your Sponsor Tonight is...

Early radio stations were not permitted to carry any "direct" advertising. This ban persisted for much of the 1920s, and as a result, the first-ever broadcast commercial, transmitted by New York's WEAF in 1922, was a rather low-key affair: a ten-minute talk by a property developer who was allowed to mention his company's name just once. However, as the original rules were relaxed, sponsored shows, promotional jingles, and other on-air sales pitches became accepted features of local and network broadcasting, and both manufacturers and program producers soon began to reap the profits.

One of the first brands to benefit from radio sponsorship was Pepsodent toothpaste, which backed *Amos 'n' Andy's* 1929 launch on NBC, and stayed with the series for many years afterward. According to broadcast historian Danny Goodwin, Pepsodent had been "floundering badly" during the late 1920s, but its sales tripled in the weeks after the show's network debut, and the company also profited from later on-air alliances with Bob Hope, Arthur Godfrey, and Art Linkletter. Meanwhile, other firms were becoming closely associated with particular program genres. Eveready batteries began sponsoring drama in 1923, subsequently launching a highly acclaimed series of monthly radio play productions, while in the following decade, support for daytime serials by Colgate-Palmolive and Procter & Gamble gave rise to the term "soap opera."

The bigger and more ambitious the show, the greater the need for a major sponsor. Oil giant Texaco began its involvement with radio in 1932, backing the weekly *Texaco Fire Chief* comedy serial, which starred Ed Wynn. In 1940, the company helped to launch *Texaco Star Theater* with Fred Allen on CBS, and the same year it embarked on one of the most substantial and long-running of all broadcast sponsorship deals when it agreed to finance a series of relays from New York's Metropolitan Opera. These live transmissions, beginning on December 7, 1940 with Mozart's *Marriage of Figaro*, were initially carried by NBC; in 1944 coverage moved to ABC, and in the late 1950s it

switched to CBS. Still on the air every Saturday afternoon, it is now broadcast over a network of selected stations worldwide.

Away from the rarefied world of the networks, smaller sponsors were continuing to support a host of popular regional radio shows. A few of these have earned themselves enduring reputations—like *King Biscuit Time*, launched at KFFA in Helena, Arkansas in 1941 to promote a local brand of flour, and famous for featuring some of the biggest names in Mississippi Delta blues, including harmonica great Sonny Boy Williamson II (1899–1965) and guitarist Robert Junior Lockwood (b. 1915). Over sixty years since its launch, the program retains a dedicated listenership.

Right: Actor and comedian Fred Allen, who presented Texaco Star Theater on radio from 1940 to 1944 with his wife, Portland Hoffa. Among the show's many distinguished guests during this period were Marlene Dietrich, Tyrone Power, Alfred Hitchcock, and Dorothy Lamour.

The Television Age Begins

"Television as a wondrous novelty," wrote a journalist for *Time* magazine in 1944, "does not begin to be television as a big industry and major public service...The prewar picture is too small, it is unclear, and it is unreliable. It blurs and wobbles, comes, and goes. To be worth a billion dollars, the television picture must be big, detailed, and true and, finally, have full color." During the war years, despite an enforced shutdown of many TV services, there was considerable progress toward delivering these requirements. Manufacturers were looking ahead to the peacetime production of receivers with larger screens—and lower price tags than the six hundred dollars charged for some pre-1941 sets. In October, 1943, program and equipment provider DuMont Laboratories installed a new 130-foot antenna atop its New York HQ on Madison Avenue, in a move to match the broadcast facilities of its rivals CBS and NBC, who operated, respectively, from the Chrysler and Empire State Buildings. And color, too, was much more than an engineer's pipe-dream. CBS had been experimenting with it since 1940, though the method used by the company for its transmission was eventually abandoned in favor of an RCA-produced system that became the industry standard.

In the meantime, monochrome pictures proved to be excitement enough for the growing numbers of new viewers who acquired TV sets—or watched them in bars, clubs, and other venues—after 1945. They were able to enjoy an extensive program schedule, including variety, music, drama, movies, and sport; NBC's relay of the Joe Louis/Billy Conn Heavyweight Championship boxing match from New York's Yankee

Above: The Chicago-based Motorola company (which remains a major innovator) was among the leading television manufacturers of the 1940s.
Like its competitors (who included Zenith, Farnsworth, and Belmont), it offered a wide range of receivers—from table-top sets to "furniture-styled" consolette and console models, which sometimes incorporated phonographs and radios in their luxurious wooden cabinets.

Stadium on June 19, 1946 was a major broadcasting milestone, attracting TV audiences of over 150,000. Transmissions were sometimes disrupted by breakdowns and other mishaps. On one occasion, an appearance by Toscanini and the NBC Symphony Orchestra had to be canceled when the lighting raised studio temperatures to unbearable levels! However, technical and production standards soon improved, in spite of the obvious difficulties caused by having to put nearly all shows out live; pre-recording was rare until the advent of magnetic videotape in the early 1950s.

Though numerous local stations had sprung up by the late 1940s, the most significant TV broadcasters were the same companies that dominated radio—NBC, CBS, and ABC. Together with DuMont, whose importance was to lessen in the early 1950s, the three majors ran networks of affiliates, distributing shows to them via AT&T coaxial cable links (these terminated at St. Louis, Missouri, making direct feeds to stations farther west impossible). Some of their material was freshly conceived to take full advantage of the new medium's possibilities (various examples are featured on the following two pages), but a good deal of it was based on existing radio formats. In September, 1948, NBC launched a TV version of *Texaco Star Theater*. It quickly became one of the greatest ratings successes of its time, earning its host, Milton Berle, the title of "Mr. Television," and its popularity was matched by that of DuMont's biggest-ever network TV show, *The Original Amateur Hour*, which first aired in January, 1948. On radio, the program had been hosted by Major Bowes, who had died two years previously; its new presenter, Ted Mack, was an

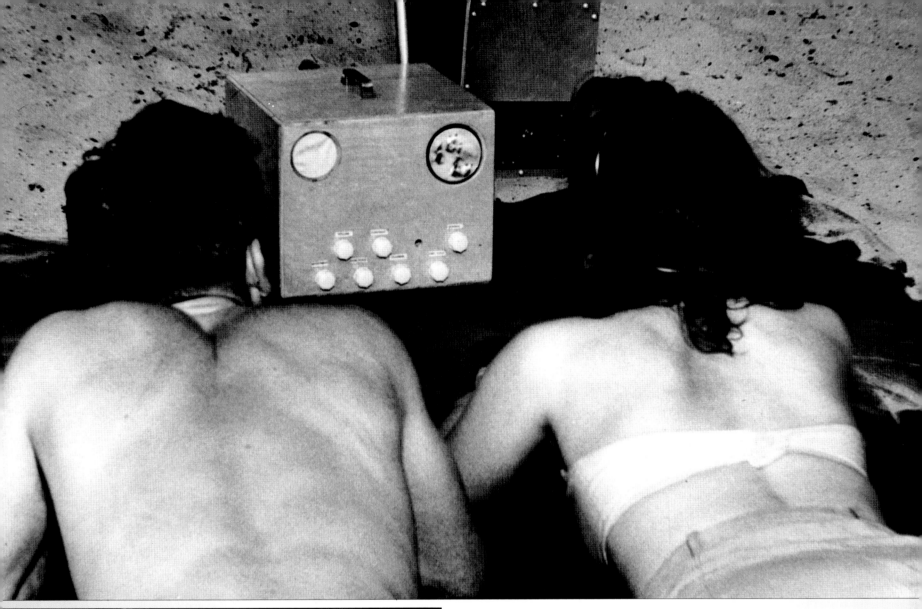

immediate hit with viewers and listeners (he also compered a sound-only version of the series for ABC), and the *Amateur Hour* remained a favorite for the next two decades. Its best-known would-be contestant was the young Elvis Presley, who failed an audition for the show in the 1950s.

1949 saw CBS's popular drama, *The Goldbergs*, make its small screen debut; the same year, NBC began a TV adaption, by original author Carlton E. Morse, of its long-running saga *One Man's Family*, while *The Lone Ranger* (starring Clayton Moore) became the first show to be specially filmed for coast-to-coast broadcast. This appropriation of top programs from radio was to continue during the new decade, and the determination among leading performers not to miss out on the "next big thing" was summed up wittily by Bob Hope, who made one of his first TV appearances on *The Star Spangled Revue* in early 1950: "All I know about television is, I want to get into it as soon as possible."

TV Makes Its Mark

By the late 1940s, some of television's classic shows were already on air, while others were just around the corner: *I Love Lucy* debuted in 1951, followed, a year later, by *Ozzie and Harriet*, which had been a radio favorite since its inception in 1944. The medium had become a magnet for fresh, highly original talent, such as Sid Caesar, a young New Yorker who had started his performing career as a saxophonist, graduating to comedy after being spotted regaling fellow musicians with his impromptu stand-up routines. In 1949, Sid starred in NBC's *Admiral Broadway Revue*—a groundbreaking but short-lived program that teamed him with comedienne Imogene Coca, and formed the basis for *Your Show of Shows*, launched in 1950. The new

Above: Betty Furness had been a moderately successful movie actress in the 1930s, but it was her television ads for Westinghouse that brought her real stardom.

Below: The radio version of Meet The Press *on the air in the mid-1940s. Like its TV spin-off, the show was broadcast weekly from Washington D.C.*

series was a massive TV hit, making Caesar and Coca household names, and boosting the reputations of its brilliant scriptwriters, who included Mel Brooks, Neil Simon, and *M*A*S*H* creator, Larry Gelbart.

Television was also being taken seriously as a news and information provider. In November, 1947, NBC began transmitting a TV version of its weekly current affairs show *Meet The Press*, heard on radio since 1945. Its on-air discussions were chaired by Lawrence Spivak, who remained at the program's helm until the mid-1970s. Another respected journalist, Douglas Edwards, first hosted CBS's nightly, fifteen-minute news broadcast in August, 1948, and was its main anchorman for the next thirteen years. The previous February, NBC had launched a

rival news show, sponsored by Camel cigarettes and presented by John Cameron Swayze, whose memorable signoff was "Glad that we could get together." Network newscasts like these were complemented by increasing coverage of regional and local events on smaller TV stations.

Money to fund this new programming was now flowing in from advertisers eager to buy time on the small screen—and to find new ways

The Howdy Doody Story

For 1940s kids with access to a TV and a taste for excitement and adventure, sci-fi serials like the DuMont network's *Captain Video* and *Tom Corbett, Space Cadet* were compulsive viewing—a touch too compulsive for some critics, like the *New York Times* correspondent who complained that television was leading "Junior [to] scorn the late-afternoon sunlight for the glamor of the darkened living room." But the most successful and enduring of all the period's children's shows was much simpler in its conception, ignoring interplanetary intrigue for the down-home charms of a wooden cowboy puppet, Howdy Doody, who made his small-screen debut on NBC in December, 1947.

According to a recent article by Howard L. Davis, Howdy Doody's distinctive voice was first created by his human sidekick, "Buffalo Bob" Smith, for a "country bumpkin" character in a mid-1940s kids' radio show, *Triple B Ranch*. The character, Elmer, always introduced himself on-air with the words "howdy doody, boys and girls," and Smith used a similar vocal styling for the marionette who was to be featured alongside him in a new TV series initially titled *Puppet Playhouse*. The program survived major teething troubles (including the abduction of the original Howdy Doody doll by puppeteer Frank Paris following a pay dispute with NBC!), and was soon renamed for its four-foot-high, freckled star. *Howdy Doody* ran for thirteen years, generating millions of dollars in merchandizing and other spin-offs, and, in 1955, was the first network TV show to be produced in color.

Above: Imogene Coca "fixes" Sid Caesar's tie during an episode of Your Show of Shows. *Coca, who died in 2001 at the age of ninety-two, was one of TV's first female comedy stars, and had worked as an actress and dancer on Broadway and in vaudeville before moving to television in the late 1940s.*

Right: "Buffalo Bob" Smith, seen in 1948 with a replica version of Howdy Doody, manufactured by the Effanbee Doll Company and sold to thousands of the TV puppet's young fans. Other Howdy Doody merchandise included cardboard cutouts, clockwork wind-ups, cookie jars (below), and lunch boxes.

of influencing viewers. Among the most persuasive campaigns of the period was the long-running series of Westinghouse ads by actress (and future consumer-rights champion) Betty Furness, who was to sell millions of refrigerators, dishwashers, and other appliances with her famous catchphrase, "You can be SURE…if it's Westinghouse," coined in 1949.

Waiting for the doors to open at New York's Radio City Music Hall in 1944.

CHAPTER SIX

IT'S THE WEEKEND

"Quality Time"

"Now, if you've ever been down to New Orleans

Then you'll understand just what I mean,

Now all through the week it's quiet as a mouse,

But on Saturday night, they go from house to house,

You don't have to pay the usual admission

If you're a cook or a waiter or a good musician.

So if you happen to be just passin' by

Stop in at the Saturday night fish fry!

"Now the folks was havin' the time of their life,

And Sam was jivin' Jimmy's wife,

And over in the corner was a beat-up grand

Being played by a big, fat piano man!

Some of the chicks wore expensive frocks,

Some of them had on bobby socks,

But everybody was nice and high

At this particular Saturday night fish fry!

"It was rockin'! It was rockin'!

You never seen such scufflin' and

shufflin' till the break of dawn!"

FROM SATURDAY NIGHT FISH FRY BY LOUIS
JORDAN, ELLIS WALSH, AND AL CARTER

Far right: *One of a series of colorful postwar ads for Wurlitzer jukeboxes. The machines offered twenty-four regularly updated musical selections, which cost customers just a nickel a number to select and play.*

Real-life Saturday nights in the 1940s rarely proved as riotous as the one in the classic Louis Jordan song quoted here, in which the partying is eventually interrupted by a police raid and the singer and his buddies end up in jail. However, for millions of hard-working Americans, then as now, weekends were a favorite time for entertainment and socializing, and music, food, drink, and dancing were all part of the fun. Jordan and his band, the Tympany Five, were an immensely popular live attraction throughout the decade—he was one of the few mainstream 1940s musicians with wide cross-racial appeal. Audiences unable to catch him in concert could hear his records, and those of other star names, on the nearly half-million jukeboxes installed in taverns, restaurants, and other premises all over the U.S.A.

Music lovers with a taste for jazz, blues, or country were also well catered-to—both in large theaters and in the smaller, hidden-away places that presented some of the latest and most exciting sounds. The atmosphere of one such Mecca in Los Angeles is conveyed by Elliot Grennard in his 1947 short story *Sparrow's Last Jump*. "The Club was a bottle joint on Central and 38th. Not much of a place for a guy *[Sparrow—a character based on jazz saxophonist Charlie 'Bird' Parker]* who's played the best locations in the country, but be-bop was too new to have a following...I know these clubs. They don't get started till one, so I got there a little after two. I took a table next to the bandstand, and...while I unwrapped my bottle I watched." Away from the big cities, as Bill C. Malone observes in his *Country Music U.S.A.*, live music venues were sometimes situated on the edge of town, enabling them to attract both rural and urban customers. In states with restrictive liquor laws, a practical location for clubs and "honky-tonks" was the county line between "dry" districts and those where alcohol could be consumed.

On Sunday mornings, many of those who had enjoyed a drink and a dance the previous evening would join their more strait-laced brothers and sisters in church. In some rural settlements, places of worship were quite literally at the center of village life. Dr. Allen H. Benson, writing in *Good Old Days* magazine, remembers "the small country church of my childhood...surrounded by farmland on three

1940
Frank Sinatra (1915–1998) begins his rise to stardom, joining Tommy Dorsey's band as a featured vocalist.

1940–1950
According to Janet Podell's *Religion in American Life*, approximately 75 percent of U.S. residents "consistently reported" they were church or synagogue members" in 1940s opinion polls.

1943
Casablanca wins three Academy Awards, including Best Picture.

1944
Louis Jordan (1908–1975) enjoys his first million-seller with G.I. Jive.

April 15, 1947
Jackie Robinson (1919–1972) makes his debut with the Brooklyn Dodgers, becoming the first black sportsman to play in major league baseball.

Above: Worshippers at an Ellis Island Catholic church in about 1950. During this period, children frequently sat or knelt in front of the pews at services.

Right: "Old time" performer Hootenanny Granny struts her stuff, to the apparent amusement of some of her backing group, at a hoedown in the mid-1940s.

sides…[and] filled with the redolence of the tall green fields of corn…[in which] small boys could play hide-and-seek until it was time for Sunday school." Churches were also focuses for community gatherings and charitable schemes, while other networks of mutual support and friendship were supplied by the "service clubs," such as the Elks, Lions, and Eagles, which thrived in most towns and cities, often offering their members medical care and sickness benefits as well as attractive dining and leisure facilities.

In this chapter, we explore some of the ways in which 1940s Americans spent their precious, all-too-brief weekends. We take a special look at two of the most popular of all pastimes, movie-going and sports, but also feature other activities, and see how the rapid expansion of youth culture (the term "teenager" was first widely used during the decade) affected and extended the already broad range of activities that were offered.

At the Movies 1940–1943

Throughout the 1940s, Hollywood excelled at realizing America's hopes, dreams, fantasies, and nightmares, fully justifying its description, by journalist Alistair Cooke, as "the most flourishing factory of popular mythology since the Greeks." At the start of the decade, *Gone With The Wind*, released in 1939, and honored with no fewer than nine Academy Awards, was still attracting huge audiences (it proved to be the world's highest-earning movie until the advent of *The Sound Of Music* twenty-five years later). However, the hottest box office draws for 1940 and 1941, according to the annual poll of films conducted by the Quigley company and published in its International Motion Picture Almanac, were the prolific Mickey Rooney, who featured as Andy Hardy in MGM's hugely popular "Hardy Family" movies and also appeared alongside Judy Garland in *Strike Up The Band* and *Babes on Broadway*, and Bette Davis, who received Oscar nominations for her star roles in *The Letter* and *The Little Foxes*.

The major newcomer to film-making in this prewar period was Orson Welles, who co-wrote, directed, and took the title role in his powerful 1941 debut, *Citizen Kane*. It was followed, a year later, by *The Magnificent Ambersons*, which suffered extensive re-editing after its premiere and was a box-office flop—setting the tone for Welles' often uneasy subsequent relationship with the Hollywood establishment. Other emerging performers included two

Above: Casablanca, released in 1942, won the Academy Award for Best Movie the following year. Its screenplay writers and its director, Michael Curtiz, also received Oscars for their work on it.

very different double-acts: a cartoon mouse called Jerry and his feline adversary Tom (originally named Jasper by his creators, William Hanna and Joe Barbera of MGM); and Abbott and Costello, who graduated from radio to star in *One Night In The Tropics* (1940). Their next picture, *Buck Privates* (1941), was a humorous look at the all-too-topical theme of enlisting in the Army (or being drafted into it). It also introduced the Andrews Sisters' famous song *The Boogie Woogie Bugle Boy of Company B.*

The studios supported the war effort with a string of patriotic (and highly profitable) pictures. As critic Robin Cross observes in Robyn Karney's *Chronicle of the Cinema* (1995), "all the stock genres could be manipulated to accommodate war-related themes. Nazi villains even rode through the ranges of the B-Western." Several World War II movies were little more than flimsy pretexts for incongruous assemblies of star names; *Stage Door Canteen*, made in 1943, somehow succeeded in bringing together, among others, violinist Yehudi Menuhin, jazzmen Benny Goodman and Count Basie, *Tarzan* star Johnny Weissmuller, Harpo Marx, and Katharine Hepburn! A few lower-budget releases were even stranger—how many home projector owners would have really wanted to purchase Castle Films' *Japs Bomb U.S.A.*, featuring "authentic footage" of the attack on Pearl Harbor, and offered cheaply on 8 and 16 mm stock? Nevertheless,

Left: Vivien Leigh, as Scarlett O'Hara, depicted on one of the original posters for Gone With The Wind. The movie was based on the novel of the same name by Margaret Mitchell (1900–1949), which was published in 1936 and won a Pulitzer Prize a year later. Shortly afterward, Mitchell sold the film rights to Hollywood producer David O. Selznick for the then astronomical sum of $50,000.

Below: Orson Welles playing Citizen Kane. The character of Kane was based on American newspaper tycoon William Randolph Hearst (1863–1951), whose famous castle in San Simeon, CA, nicknamed "The Ranch," corresponds to Kane's "Xanadu." Welles and co-writer Herman J. Mankiewicz were awarded an Oscar for the film's screenplay.

some productions—notably the classic *Casablanca* (1942), starring Humphrey Bogart and Ingrid Bergman—succeeded brilliantly in weaving the war into the essence of their plots, while other film-makers, following the example of Charlie Chaplin's prewar attack on Hitler, *The Great Dictator,* deployed comedy as an effective weapon against Nazism. Perhaps the most distinguished example of this approach was *To Be Or Not To Be* (1942), directed by German émigré Ernst Lubitsch, and starring Jack Benny and Carole Lombard, who was to die in a plane crash in Nevada shortly after completing the movie.

At the Movies 1944–1950

Despite wartime austerities, Hollywood seemed to be in good artistic and financial shape through most of the 1940s. Exciting new performers were emerging, like the nineteen-year-old Lauren Bacall, who thrilled audiences when she appeared alongside Humphrey Bogart in *To Have and Have Not* in 1944. The same year saw the release of *Meet Me In St. Louis*, starring Judy Garland and directed by her future husband, Vincente Minnelli, who had made his name a year earlier with the all-black musical, *Cabin In The Sky*; and Elizabeth Taylor's impressive portrayal of Velvet Brown in *National Velvet*. Meanwhile, seasoned movie-makers such as Alfred Hitchcock and Billy Wilder, whose *film noir* masterpiece, *Double Indemnity*, was nominated for six Oscars in 1944, were refining their skills and expanding the range and subtlety of film-making. And, to the delight of hard-nosed producers like Harry Warner of Warner Brothers, who once commented that "pictures are just expensive dreams," profits and audience figures were (temporarily) up. Figures quoted by David Parkinson in his 1996 *History of Film* show that, by 1946, about 100 million Americans were going to the movies each week, generating box-office revenues of some $1.7 million.

Above: *Lauren Bacall (b. 1924) in* To Have and Have Not. *Its director, Howard Hawks, had summoned Bacall to Hollywood after seeing her in Harper's Bazaar magazine, for which she been modeling.*

Above: *A publicity shot of Elizabeth Taylor (b. 1932) from the mid-1940s. An American born in London, she got her first movie roles following her family's move to Los Angeles at the start of World War II.*

Above: *After working with her two sisters in vaudeville, Judy Garland (1922–1969) made her Hollywood debut as a teenager. She quickly found fame and fortune (though seldom happiness) there.*

However, ominous clouds were gathering over the industry. In 1944, *Gone With the Wind* co-star Olivia de Havilland sued Warner Brothers over its refusal to release her from a "personal service contract" that had been extended beyond its nominal seven-year length by the use of complex "suspension" clauses. Similar contracts were employed by Warner's competitors, and a court ruling that De Havilland's was illegal effectively ended the tight control—amounting to virtual ownership—that the big studios had exercised over some of their most famous artists. There were further blows in store for the movie bosses. In 1945 and 1946, two disputes, the first of which involved mass picketing and violent attempts at strikebreaking, led to substantial pay increases for Hollywood craft workers; and in 1948, a legal reverse deprived production companies of their lucrative monopoly on film distribution (see pages 40–41). During this period, television was also beginning to reduce theater attendances.

These difficulties, and the notorious H.U.A.C. inquiry (described on pages 26–27) leading to the imprisonment of the "Hollywood Ten" and the blacklisting of left-wing performers and production staff, did not put a stop to quality movie-making. Films such as *Miracle on 34th Street*,

Above: *A scene from* On The Town *(1949), featuring (L–R) Jules Munshin, Frank Sinatra, and Gene Kelly. Kelly also directed and choreographed the movie, in collaboration with Stanley Donen; the score was by Leonard Bernstein.*

released in 1947 and starring Edmund Gwenn, Maureen O'Hara, and Natalie Wood, and the superb *On The Town*—a 1949 Oscar-winning vehicle for Gene Kelly and Frank Sinatra—were critical and box-office successes. There were also continuing technical breakthroughs, like the development of the Eastmancolor system, launched in 1950 as a rival to Technicolor, and the introduction, a few years later, of Cinerama and Cinemascope. But Hollywood's once-progressive ethos had been replaced by a conservatism symbolized by the influence of the right-wing Motion Picture Alliance for the Preservation of American Ideals, whose members included John Wayne, Walt Disney, and Gary Cooper. According to Joel Kotkin and Paul Grabowicz's 1982 book, *California Inc.*, this group's ascendancy reflected a growing preference in the late 1940s and early '50s for "movies [that] stuck to the traditional American themes. It was the era of the good guys versus the bad guys, the black hats against the white hats," and of a "nationalistic consciousness" that was to dominate Hollywood for many years to come.

Right: Christian Dior's revolutionary 1947 fashion collection established his reputation on both sides of the Atlantic. Among its highlights was this green velvet, full-skirted "Prince Igor" coat, with three-quarter length sleeves, slanted pockets decorated with gold and silver embroidery, and a characteristically tightly belted waist. The coat's leopardskin cuffs are matched by an elegant pillbox hat made from the same material.

Above: A 1946 photograph showing off two summer dresses created by Claire McCardell. A graduate of New York's Parsons School of Design, McCardell launched her "own-label" line of casualwear in 1940, and retained a lifelong commitment to (as she put it) "design[ing] for the lives American women lead today."

Women's Fashions

Throughout the years of wartime rationing, many movie-goers would have gazed enviously at the glamorous costumes worn by the stars on the big screen. With the disappearance of French *haute couture* from American stores, actresses and Hollywood stylists became the main arbiters of fashion. Their outfits were widely copied by home dressmakers, working from published patterns and substituting readily available (usually synthetic) materials for the original silks and satins. Inevitably, though, some more elaborate items proved impossible to re-create—like the cantilevered brassieres specially made for Jane Russell in *The Outlaw* (1943) by the picture's director, airplane mogul Howard Hughes!

The temporary absence of Parisian fashions also boosted the status and confidence of U.S. designers, who had been overshadowed by their European counterparts before the war. Between 1941 and 1945, a distinctively American style of women's clothing began to emerge; it displayed a stylish practicality very different from the elaboration and constriction of French *couture,* and was typified by the work of Claire McCardell (1905–1958), whose casual yet smart dresses (which she often modeled herself) rapidly became best-sellers. McCardell, together with other pioneers such as Pauline Trigère and Tina Leser, dominated the U.S. ready-to-wear market in the late 1940s. Their distinguished contemporaries included Norman Norell (1900–1972), whose outfits have been described as "the realization of every elegant woman's dreams," and Hattie Carnegie (1886–1956), who created not only high fashion but the uniforms for the Women's Army Corps, and even the habits for an order of nuns!

The French fashion industry gradually recovered from the tribulations of war and occupation, announcing its return to international influence with the *"Théâtre de la Mode"* exhibition that visited New York in 1946 (see pages 30–31). However, its first major postwar breakthrough came a year later, when Christian Dior (1905–1957) presented his first *haute couture* collection in Paris. Dior's designs were a radical departure from the austerities once demanded by rationing. His fuller, longer skirts, supported by petticoats as they spread elegantly outward from tightly cinched waistlines, were almost profligate in their use of fabric. They

were combined with soft-shouldered, snugly bodiced jackets to create what he called a "flower-like" quality, which contrasted sharply with the plain, utilitarian appearance of women's wartime garments.

Dubbed "the New Look" by *Vogue* magazine, Dior's debut collection brought him international acclaim, and in 1948, he opened a store selling his "own-label" ready-to-wear in New York, although many American customers were happy to make do with the cheaper copies of his suits provided by less exclusive retailers. These outlets also offered cut-price imitations of other high-fashion clothing, and by the end of the decade, almost any woman planning a night on the town could be sure of finding an affordable outfit that would made her look—and feel—like a million dollars.

The Sporting Year

By the 1940s, many of the principal fixtures in the modern U.S. sports calendar were well established, though some of the rules governing them were changing. Until 1946, for example, the Pacific Coast Conference ("Pac-10"), whose college football champions appeared in the famous Pasadena Rose Bowl game every New Year's Day, had always chosen their own opponents from among a group of more easterly university teams. However, that year it was decided to play all subsequent Rose Bowl games between the top "Big Ten" (Western Conference) team and its Pac-10 counterpart. This resulted in an exciting Illinois-UCLA clash on January 1, 1947 (the locals lost 14–45), and attracted larger crowds and radio audiences than ever before. The Rose Bowl had been broadcast on NBC since 1925, and in 1948 it was

Above: Ned Day, America's best-known bowling champion, endorses Camel cigarettes in this magazine ad, which first appeared in 1951.

carried on local television for the first time. The most consistently successful Rose Bowl team of the decade was that of the University of Southern California, victorious in 1940, 1944, and 1945.

College football had rather more fans than its professional equivalent, which was dominated by the National Football League, with occasional competition from other, usually short-lived groupings. At this time, the NFL's income from franchises and broadcasting rights was still comparatively limited, and it lacked the kind of blockbuster finale to its season that the January Super Bowl (launched in 1966) was later to provide.

Despite these drawbacks, there was already a rapidly growing following for its games, which culminated in a mid-December Championship Game won by the Chicago Bears in 1940, 1941, 1943, and 1946.

Basketball and ice hockey were significant attractions during the remaining winter months, but soon spectators' thoughts were turning to spring and summer, and the return of the main seasons for baseball (discussed separately on the next two pages) and horseracing. For devotees of the "Sport of Kings," the decade was one of mixed emotions. The much-loved Seabiscuit, whose victories of the 1930s had, in the words of journalist Rob Hardy, "beat[en] Roosevelt, Hitler, and Mussolini in

Left: Cleveland Browns' fullback Tony Adamie is unable to prevent Walt Clay of the LA Dons scoring a touchdown in this 1948 NFL Western Division football match. In spite of Clay's efforts, the Browns eventually won 31–14.

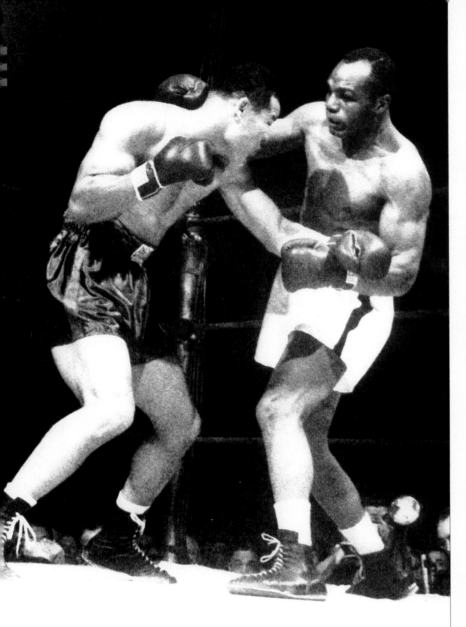

contenders like Pancho Gonzales, Frank Parker, and Pauline Betz.

Fall brought the start of the pro and college football seasons, and while, week after week, faithful supporters would turn out to support their favorite teams, one special match—the Army/Navy football game, contested by cadets from West Point and the U.S. Naval Academy on the Saturday after Thanksgiving—drew more widespread attention. This historic meeting had taken place annually since 1890, and was first televised from its then-regular venue, Philadelphia's Municipal Stadium, in 1945. The Army was victorious that year, and in four of the other games between 1940 and 1950.

Boxing lies outside the seasonal round of sporting events described above, but its huge popularity led to extensive newspaper and broadcast coverage (and generous purses) for every important fight of the period. One of the greatest of all 1940s boxers was "Brown Bomber" Joe Louis, who won the world heavyweight championship in Chicago in 1937—the first black man to do so in nearly three decades. Louis' thrilling defenses of his title over the next ten years brought him immense fame and respect. But nevertheless, a panel of experts assembled in 1999 by Associated Press named another distinguished figure, middle-, and welterweight champion, Sugar Ray Robinson, "Fighter of the Century." Robinson delivered over a hundred knockouts in his lengthy career; among his most memorable encounters in the ring were a series of bouts with arch-rival Jake LaMotta (a.k.a. the "Bronx Bull") during the 1940s and early 1950s.

amount of newspaper coverage," retired in 1940 after coming first in the Santa Anita Handicap at Arcadia, California. He died in 1947, and the same year saw the passing of Man o' War, who, in his prime, had shattered a succession of track and world records. But new equine stars were emerging, notably Whirlaway, Count Fleet, and Assault, all holders of the coveted Triple Crown, awarded to champions who win three classic races—the Kentucky Derby, the Preakness Stakes (raced at the Pimlico course in Baltimore, Maryland), and New York's Belmont Stakes—in a single season. Citation, the first horse to earn over $1 million during his racing career, joined this select group in 1948.

Summer also saw premier tennis events such as the U.S. National Championship, hosted by the West Side Tennis Club at Forest Hills, Queens, New York—although its entrants (like competitors at all the game's other major tournaments) had to be amateurs. Several former champions, including Brucé Barnes and Bobby Riggs, turned professional in the 1940s; their places were taken by younger

Top left: Joe Louis, en route for victory at New York's Madison Square Garden on December 5, 1947, lands a punch on challenger "Jersey" Joe Walcott.

Above: The Pimlico race track at Baltimore, Maryland in May, 1943. The course's celebrated Preakness Stakes was won that year by Count Fleet.

Baseball

"I started playing when I was eight years old. With a sock ball. Do you know what that is? That's an old sock that you fold up tight as you can and then get your mother to sew up. We used a broomstick for a bat. […] I occupied myself as a boy by playing baseball. All summer long, and then every other chance I could, between school time…I always had my mind set on being a ballplayer." TED LYONS, QUOTED IN *BASEBALL—WHEN THE GRASS WAS REAL* BY DONALD HONIG (1975)

For ambitious youngsters such as Lyons, who, in 1923, went straight from college in Waco, Texas, to become a pitcher for the Chicago White Sox (and stayed with them for over two decades), baseball offered a fast track to fame and fortune. The game was hugely popular and impressively organized (even boasting its own Commissioner, Federal Judge Kenesaw Mountain Landis), and top teams were able to scour schools and universities for talented players, and to pay them generously—even during the Depression years. Second baseman Billy Herman was recruited by the Chicago Cubs in 1931; the next year, as he told Donald Honig, "I made $7,000, which was a ton of money then. I came from a big family, and some of my brothers were struggling just to earn eating money."

However, even salaries like this were eclipsed by the sums commanded by baseball's biggest names. In 1930, the legendary George Herman "Babe" Ruth was receiving $80,000 a year from the New York Yankees, while the man often regarded as his heir-apparent, Joe DiMaggio, made over $700,000 during his thirteen seasons (1936–1942, 1946–1951) with the same team. The Yankees enjoyed consistent success throughout the 1930s, and did even better in the following decade. This was despite the retirement of Babe Ruth, and the loss of another all-time great, Lou Gehrig, who died from a rare degenerative illness on June 2, 1941—a few months before the Yankees beat National Leaguers Brooklyn 4–1 in the World Series, which they were to win again in 1943, 1947, 1949, and 1950.

After Pearl Harbor, travel restrictions and the drafting of many top sportsmen caused inevitable problems to the leagues, though any notion of suspending the professional game for the duration of hostilities was effectively quashed by President Roosevelt, who wrote to Judge Landis in early 1942 that "I honestly feel…it would be best for the country to keep baseball going. […] Even if the actual quality [of] the teams is lowered by the greater use of older players, this will not dampen the popularity of the sport." As FDR predicted, baseball games (many of which were now being played in the evening to enable day shift workers to see them) provided a welcome, if temporary, respite from the rigors of war. Nevertheless, standards of play in 1942–1945 were often disappointing. When asked for his opinion on the outcome of the 1945 World Series between the Chicago Cubs and the Detroit Tigers, one leading journalist, Warren Brown, commented acidly that he felt neither of the finalists was capable of victory!

Below: Joe DiMaggio (1914–1999) hits out for the New York Yankees at a home game in 1946—his first year back with the team following three seasons' absence in the Army.

Above: The official New York Giants program and scorecard for 1949. The cover photo shows the team's ballpark, the Polo Grounds, which they occupied from 1911 until its closure in 1963.

Jackie Robinson— Breaking the "Color Line"

Jack Roosevelt Robinson (1919–1972) was born in Georgia but brought up in Southern California, where he demonstrated his outstanding ability as an all-round athlete at school and later at UCLA. After wartime service as an army lieutenant, he joined the Kansas City Monarchs baseball team in 1945. The Monarchs were a mainstay of the Negro League, but the racial segregation which had been a fact of life in professional baseball since the nineteenth century meant that they and other black teams could not compete against white clubs in the major (American and National) leagues. It was also unheard of for individual black players, however talented, to become members of AL and NL teams.

This bad old tradition, however, was shortly to be swept away. Jackie Robinson's skills had been spotted by Branch Rickey, manager of the Brooklyn Dodgers, a leading National League side, and, in late 1945, Rickey signed him to the Montreal Royals, a farm club for the Dodgers. Robinson played brilliantly with the Royals the following year, and Rickey— though acutely aware of the controversy his actions would cause—signed him with the Dodgers at the start of the 1947 season. Once again, the new recruit excelled on the field, while his extraordinary forbearance and dignity in the face of racist abuse from fans (and some fellow sportsmen) helped to change attitudes and facilitate further integration within baseball. Less than three months after his Brooklyn debut, another former Negro Leaguer, Larry Doby, was taken on by the Cleveland Indians; and in 1948, the same club hired Leroy "Satchel" Paige, a black pitcher commended by Joe DiMaggio as "the best and fastest I've ever faced."

Robinson himself stayed with the Dodgers until his retirement from the game in 1956; he had been awarded the coveted title of the National League's "Most Valued Player" seven years earlier. He devoted much of the rest of his life to civil rights-related causes.

The situation improved with the return from military service of stars like the Tigers' Hank Greenberg, the Yankees' DiMaggio, and Stan Musial of the St. Louis Cardinals; and baseball was soon attracting growing numbers of spectators at home and (increasingly) on television. It also gained a new Commissioner, Kentucky Senator Albert "Happy" Chandler, after the death of Judge Landis in 1944. But its most significant postwar transformation took place in 1947, when, for the first time, a black player, Jackie Robinson, took his place with a major league team, the Brooklyn Dodgers, in a move that was soon to have profound consequences for sports and society in general.

Left and above left: Jackie Robinson's height (he was almost six feet tall), agility, and speed were major assets to his team, the Brooklyn Dodgers. In 1950, at the peak of his playing career with them, he starred in a Hollywood movie that told his life story, and featured re-creations of some of his most outstanding moments on the field.

Golf and Bowling

Football and baseball attracted a mass following, but were only played by those young and energetic enough to sustain the games' frenetic pace. When participating in sports, many adults preferred a combination of gentle exercise, relaxation, pleasant surroundings, and agreeable company, and often found it at two of the nation's most popular recreational venues—its golf links and bowling alleys.

According to information from the University of Chicago, there were over 4,500 golf courses in the U.S.A. by the start of the 1940s. These ranged from prestigious facilities owned by private clubs to humbler municipal links whose green fees were well within the reach of less affluent players. Some of these

Above: This one's going straight in…a keen young golfer concentrates on lining up a putt at the juvenile golf course in Hershey, Pennsylvania, while his family look on. The photograph dates from about 1950.

courses, particularly in the Southern states, operated openly racist policies that excluded black golfers. A recent article in the Fort Worth, Texas *Star-Telegram* recalls that, until the mid-1960s, African-Americans were permitted to use the city's golf courses on just one day a year— June 19 ("Juneteenth," the date on which Union troops liberated Texan slaves in 1865). At other times, they were obliged to play in schoolyards, or at a makeshift course at Greenway Park, where, in the words of one patron, Oscar Haswell, "there were no greens, no fairways, no fancy stuff, just a couple of coffee cups and a stick with a rag on it for a flag."

Sadly, the only way in which black enthusiasts like Haswell could have experienced adequate golfing facilities would have been to work as a caddy at an affluent white club. Such venues were becoming steadily more sophisticated during the 1940s, acquiring impressive new equipment (from motorized golfing carts to the ingenious "aerifiers" used by greenskeepers to improve the quality of the turf), and sometimes modifying their original layouts to match the powerful capabilities of the latest balls and drivers. And, although most weekend players resisted the temptation, the dedicated amateur could easily

spend a small fortune on clubs, tuition fees, clothing, and a growing range of golf-related publications—from books of tips by the stars to magazines such as *Golf World* and *Golf Journal*, launched respectively in 1947 and 1948.

1940s bowling was a rather simpler affair. Little or no personal equipment was required, and the alleys where it took place were resolutely "lo-tech" places, which still employed human "pinboys" to reset knocked-down pins; automatic pinspotting machines were not introduced until the early 1950s. The sport had long since shaken off its former, shady reputation (several cities had banned it in the nineteenth century for encouraging gambling), and was now favored by family groups and teams from churches, service clubs, and businesses, who often enjoyed a leisurely drink and a chat at the alley before or after a game.

However, this sometimes gentle pastime also had a more competitive edge. Bodies such as the American Bowling Congress and the Bowling Proprietors' Association of America organized regional and national tournaments (sponsors included Stroh beer and the *Chicago Tribune*), and a handful of professional bowlers became household names. One leading figure, B.P.A.A. champion Ned Day (1911–1971), appeared in his own series of bowling-related films, and even gave a display of his skills to President Truman at the White House in 1948. Promotional activities like these, plus increasing levels of TV coverage, helped to raise the profile of the sport, and before long, thousands of new alleys were springing up to cope with the resultant increase in demand—especially from the youngsters who began swelling attendance figures from the mid-1950s onward.

Right: A moment of pure joy for a smartly dressed teenager from Jamaica High School, New York, as he celebrates his strike at a local bowling alley. Large numbers of Americans had been taking up the sport since the war.

The New "Teen-Age"

By the mid-1940s, most American adolescents were staying in high school until graduation. Little more than ten years earlier, a substantial proportion of seventeen or eighteen year-olds would have been at work, and some might have even had children of their own, but typical postwar teenagers were blissfully free of such encumbrances. They lived at home, could do much as they pleased outside school hours, and often had considerable amounts of spending money, thanks to generous parental allowances and wages from part-time jobs. No large group of under-twenty-ones had ever enjoyed such economic power and relative autonomy, and the adult world could not ignore their aspirations and tastes, although it sometimes struggled to come to terms with them.

Schools themselves were obliged to respond to the wishes of older pupils seeking increased responsibility and more "grown-up" leisure facilities. "Teen councils" were given some influence over rules and decisions, and "teen canteens," where kids could socialize after class and on weekends, became widely popular. One such canteen opened at Linton-Stockton School, Indiana, in 1945; admission cost a dime, and, according to a former student, girls (wearing "skirts, sweaters, and pennyloafers") and boys (clad in "dress pants and nice shirts") would flock there to dance, consume snacks and soft drinks, and play ping-pong and pool. Like similar set-ups all over the country, it was run by a committee of kids, teachers, and volunteers, and provided a safe, strictly supervised environment for teenage recreation.

However, many youngsters—notably the fashion-conscious female fans of 1940s swing music known as "bobbysoxers"—wanted greater excitement than school-sanctioned activities could supply. Away from the chaperoned canteens, some of them danced the Lindy Hop and the Suzie Q with (in the words of Grace Palladino, author of *Teenagers—An American History*) "a little too much thigh…for adult comfort." They disconcerted parents and teachers by using "jive talk," derived from black jazzmen's slang. And at concerts by their musical idol, Frank Sinatra, their behavior reached levels of intensity rivalling the hysterical devotion of 1960s Beatles fans. Bobbysoxers screamed for Sinatra, tried to pull hairs from his head, and—on at least one occasion—threw their underwear onto the stage at his shows.

Such obsessions attracted sharp condemnation from some quarters. But, like other teenage enthusiasms, the swing craze proved to be a harmless affair that brought none of the dire consequences (delinquency, promiscuity) predicted by the doomsayers. Inevitably, though, the youth market gradually changed its tastes, and the music industry's efforts to retain the allegiance (and the dollars) of this affluent, fickle group of consumers led to the emergence of a succession of new stars and styles, some of which are examined overleaf.

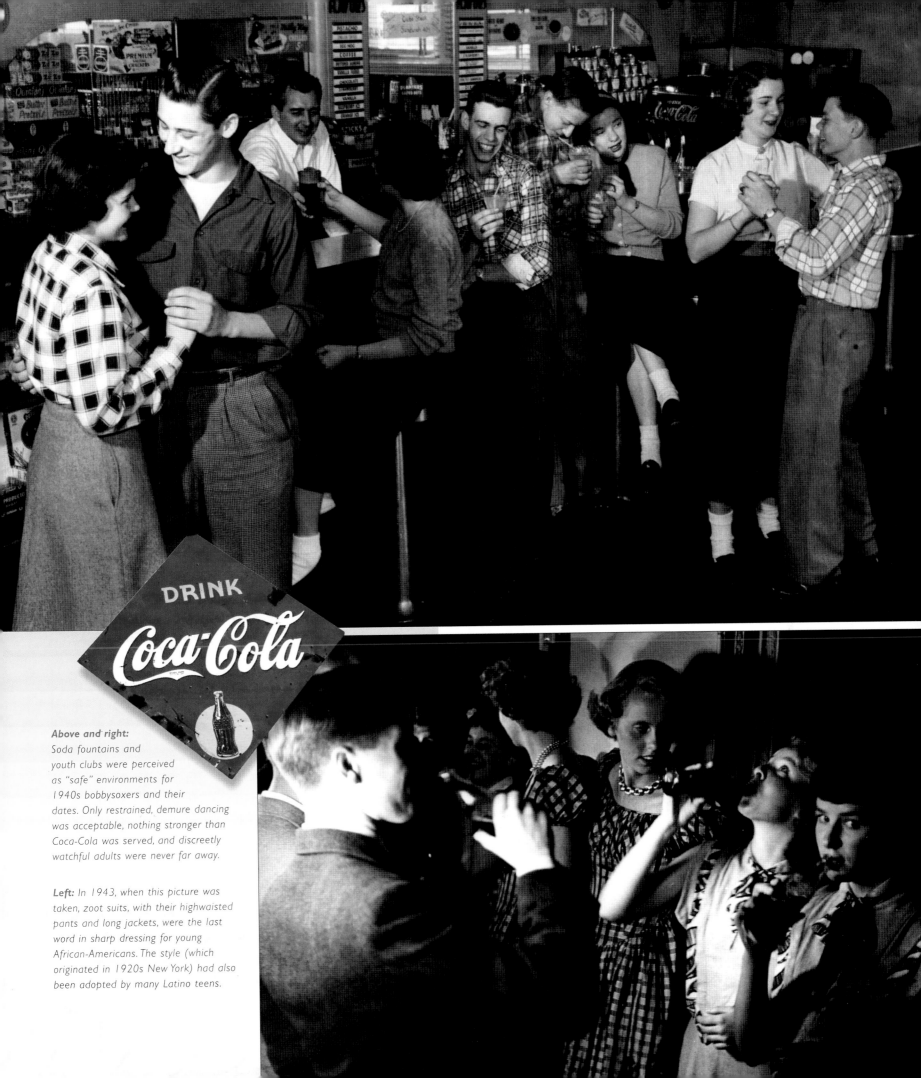

DRINK Coca-Cola

Above and right:
Soda fountains and
youth clubs were perceived
as "safe" environments for
1940s bobbysoxers and their
dates. Only restrained, demure dancing
was acceptable, nothing stronger than
Coca-Cola was served, and discreetly
watchful adults were never far away.

Left: In 1943, when this picture was
taken, zoot suits, with their highwaisted
pants and long jackets, were the last
word in sharp dressing for young
African-Americans. The style (which
originated in 1920s New York) had also
been adopted by many Latino teens.

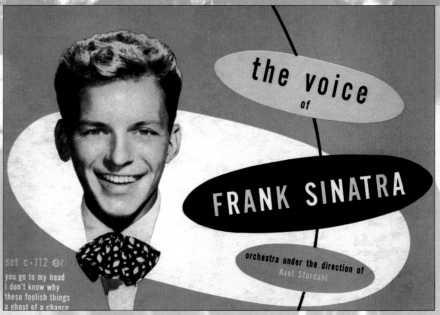

Left: "Jump blues" star Louis Jordan (1908–1975) made music whose sparkling wit and infectious rhythms transcended racial barriers. He once gleefully commented that "I made just as much money off white people as I did colored…I could play a white joint this week and a colored next."

Above: After establishing himself as a solo singer (and teenage hearthrob), Frank Sinatra had rather less success in the late 1940s, partly as a result of poorly chosen songs and arrangements. It took a move to the Capitol label in 1953 to put him back on the right musical track.

The Changing Face of '40s Music

On July 20, 1940, *Billboard,* America's leading music business journal, published its first modern-style sales chart for record releases. At number one was *I'll Never Smile Again* by the Tommy Dorsey Orchestra, with vocals by Frank Sinatra. Like nearly all big band singers at this time, Sinatra was billed below his leader, although his growing reputation was soon to make him the major attraction at Dorsey concerts; just two years later, he left the band to start a solo career. Over the next few years, "staff" vocalists with other ensembles, including Perry Como, Kay Starr, and—a little later—Rosemary Clooney, also struck out on their own, and gradually, individual singers and smaller groups began to replace the orchestras (most of which struggled to survive after the war) in the pop charts.

Radio listeners could keep abreast of these developments by tuning into *Your Hit Parade,* a Saturday night institution, broadcast weekly at 9 pm on the CBS (and, subsequently, NBC) networks throughout the decade. Sponsored by Lucky Strike cigarettes, it presented studio performances of the numbers deemed by its producers to be "the best sellers on sheet music and phonograph records, [and] the songs most heard on the air and most played on the automatic coin machines." Many stars guested on the show, and Frank Sinatra himself had two lengthy stints as one of its featured vocalists in 1943–1944 and 1947–1949. But by the late 1940s, Frank was increasingly unhappy with much of the music heard on the program. In an outspoken interview for *Metronome* magazine in February, 1948, he observed that "the popular songs of the day…[have] become so decadent, they're so bloodless. As a singer…I've been looking for wonderful pieces of music in the popular vein—what they call Tin Pan Alley songs…Outside of production material, show tunes, you can't find a thing."

Above: *The Ink Spots' sweet four-part vocal harmonies brought them a string of best-selling records in the 1930s and 1940s, including* That's When Your Heartaches Begin *(1941), which was later famously covered by Elvis Presley.*

These comments, which coincided with a relatively lean patch in Sinatra's own career, should be taken with a grain of salt, but it was true that nothing very substantial had yet emerged to fill the void in the pop charts left by the decline of the big bands. There was, however, far more artistic vitality outside the musical mainstream; *Billboard* had already acknowledged this by launching a "Harlem Hit Parade" (later renamed the "race" and "rhythm and blues" chart) in 1942, and a country and western chart two years later. Louis Jordan frequently dominated the R&B listings, and among other "race" best-sellers were Wynonie Harris, whose *Good Rockin' Tonight* (1948) lit up many a weekend party, and piano player and singer Amos Milburn, whose classics included *Hold Me Baby* (1948) and *Bad Bad Whiskey* (1950). Meanwhile, Hank Williams was the toast of the honky-tonks with *Lovesick Blues,* which topped the country charts in 1949, and the following year, Patti Page's *Tennessee Waltz* proved even more successful, going on to become one of the genre's greatest-ever hits.

Thanks to a proliferation of local radio stations, it was now possible for more listeners than ever before to hear and enjoy country and rhythm and blues records. Their impact was enormous, and the cross-fertilization of the two styles, as country musicians such as Bill Haley (who was working as a disc jockey for WPWA in Brookhaven, Pennsylvania in the late 1940s) began borrowing some of the attitude and urgency of R&B, would eventually lead to the explosive fusion of rock and roll. In the meantime, though, despite the dissatisfaction voiced by Frank Sinatra, most audiences could be reasonably content with what was currently on offer—whether they preferred a quiet evening in, soothed by the mellow sounds of a crooner, or a Louis Jordan-style Saturday night fish fry, with drums, saxes, and a "big fat piano man" to help the good times roll.

The lights of Broadway brightening a winter night in New York, January, 1941.

ON STAGE
AND IN PRINT

Culture on Broadway

...and Beyond

"So I wish you first a
Sense of theatre; only
Those who love illusion
And know it will go far:
Otherwise we spend our
Lives in a confusion
Of what we say and do with
Who we really are."

FROM MANY HAPPY RETURNS (FOR JOHN RETTGER)
BY W.H. AUDEN (1907–1973)

hen British-born poet W.H. Auden wrote *Many Happy Returns* in 1942, his recently adopted home city of New York was the focus of a remarkable artistic and literary scene that continued to flourish throughout the war years and beyond. Anyone sharing Auden's "sense of theatre" would have found much to delight them on Broadway during this period, including the premieres of major new plays by Eugene O'Neill, Tennessee Williams, and Arthur Miller. The decade was also a golden age for musicals, with outstanding successes by both established and emerging talent. Richard Rodgers' songwriting partnership with Oscar Hammerstein II led to the triumphs of *Oklahoma!* and *South Pacific* (these and other key shows are covered in more detail on the next two pages); and in 1942, the young Leonard Bernstein's *On The Town* was launched at Broadway's Adelphi Theatre, where it ran for over four hundred performances.

European émigrés such as Auden, who became an American citizen in 1946, played an important role in creating this unique cultural climate. In 1941, *Paul Bunyan*, the operetta he wrote with English composer Benjamin Britten (a U.S. resident from 1939 till 1942), was premiered at New York's Columbia University. The piece received a lukewarm reception, and was not revived until shortly before Britten's death in 1976, but it led to other operatic collaborations for Auden, most notably with the Russian-born Igor Stravinsky, for whose opera *The Rake's Progress* (1951) he and his partner, Chester Kallman, provided the libretto. Auden's already distinguished reputation was further enhanced by the publication, in 1947, of *The Age of Anxiety*, a hundred-page work whose title-page carried an ominous Latin quotation from the Catholic Mass for the Dead. The poem won the 1948 Pulitzer Prize, and it went on to inspire Leonard Bernstein's second symphony, also named *The Age of Anxiety*, which was premiered in 1949 by the Boston Symphony Orchestra, with the composer at the piano. The conductor and dedicatee, Serge Koussevitzky, had been displeased with Bernstein, his former student, for his earlier excursion into showbusiness with *On The Town*, and he was anxious to persuade him to return to "serious" composition, though, fortunately, his advice did not prevent Lenny from creating his finest, and most enduring, popular musical, *West Side Story*, in 1957.

Left: Jessica Tandy (foreground) playing Blanche Du Bois in the original Broadway production of Tennessee Williams' A Streetcar Named Desire at the Ethel Barrymore Theatre in 1947. On her left are Marlon Brando (Stanley Kowalski) and Kim Hunter (Stella Kowalski). The play, which ran for two years, was directed by Elia Kazan.

1940s TIMELINE

March 31, 1943
Oklahoma! by Richard Rodgers and Oscar Hammerstein II opens on Broadway.

October 30, 1944
The Martha Graham Dance Company gives the first performance of Aaron Copland's *Appalachian Spring* at the Library of Congress in Washington D.C.

December 26, 1944
Tennessee Williams' play *The Glass Menagerie* opens at Chicago's Civic Theatre. It later transfers to Broadway.

October 9, 1946
First performance of *The Iceman Cometh* by Eugene O'Neill at New York's Martin Beck Theatre.

January 29, 1947
Arthur Miller's *All My Sons* is premiered at the Coronet Theatre on Broadway.

Numerous other settlers from overseas—among them the conductor Leopold Stokowski, whose apparently Slavonic name disguised his British ancestry—helped to shape the course of twentieth century American music. But perhaps the most significant contributors to its development were the German Jews who fled from Nazism in the 1930s and early '40s. Their special achievements are assessed later in this chapter, as is the work of some of the U.S.A.'s leading pre- and postwar novelists and authors.

The 1940s were also an exciting time for the visual arts, with painters as diverse as Edward Hopper and the Abstract Expressionist Jackson Pollock working and exhibiting in New York. And, in October, 1941, America's largest piece of public sculpture, the massive carvings of Presidents Washington, Lincoln, Jefferson, and Theodore Roosevelt on Mount Rushmore in South Dakota, were finally completed by Lincoln Borglum. His father, Gutzon, who began the project in 1927, had died a few months before.

Above: Putting the finishing touches to the National Memorial at Mount Rushmore, South Dakota, in 1941.

Below: British-born conductor Leopold Stokowski, who had worked in the U.S.A. since 1905, at a wartime rehearsal.

Stage Musicals

Many of the greatest prewar Broadway musicals were written by a handful of individual composers (Jerome Kern, Cole Porter, Irving Berlin, Harry Warren, and Harold Arlen) and established partnerships (George and Ira Gershwin, Richard Rodgers, and Lorenz [Larry] Hart). In the late 1930s, however, this relatively stable scene was beginning to change. George Gershwin died, at the age of only thirty-eight, in 1937, just two years after he and his brother Ira had created the opera, *Porgy and Bess*. During the same period, Jerome Kern was devoting most of his creative energies to Hollywood. His final stage musical, *Very Warm For May* (1939),

Above: Leonard Bernstein, choreographer Jerome Robbins, Betty Comden, and Adolph Green creating On The Town.

featuring the classic song *All The Things You Are*, proved to be, in the words of critic Joel Bernstein, "a dismal flop," and he did not live to see the successful 1945 Broadway revival of *Showboat*, which he had written with Oscar Hammerstein II eighteen years before. Meanwhile, Hammerstein himself had begun working with Richard Rodgers, whose relationship with Larry Hart had foundered, largely as a result of the lyricist's alcoholism, after the completion of *Pal Joey* (1940) and *By Jupiter* (1942); Hart died in 1943.

These regroupings—as well as the emergence of fresh talent like Leonard Bernstein and his *On The Town* collaborators Betty Comden and Adolph Green—led to exciting new developments on Broadway, where Rodgers and Hammerstein's *Oklahoma!*, the first fruits of their partnership, opened at the St. James Theatre on March 31, 1943. During its earlier, out of town tryouts, the show had undergone several last-minute alterations, as well as a change of name (it had originally been titled *Away We Go!*) The fine-tuning and careful preparation clearly paid off; *Oklahoma!* was a triumph at the box-office and with the critics, going on to win a Pulitzer Prize, spawning the first original cast recording ever made of a stage musical, and running on Broadway for a record 2,212 performances. Its success raised expectations for Rodgers and Hammerstein's next show, *Carousel* (1945), to dauntingly high levels,

and almost inevitably, the new piece did not enjoy the same acclaim as its predecessor, though *South Pacific*, their third collaboration, proved to be another blockbuster when it was premiered four years later.

Musical historian John Kenrick echoes many other experts when he describes *Oklahoma!* as "the first fully integrated musical play, using every song and dance to develop the characters or the plot," adding that "after *Oklahoma!*, the musical would never be the same." Its example certainly stimulated a change of direction for Irving Berlin, who, in late 1945, received a commission from Rodgers and Hammerstein (acting as producers) to write a show based on the career of Annie Oakley, following the sudden death of their first choice for composer, Jerome Kern. Berlin completed his score in just a few weeks, and *Annie Get Your Gun* opened in May, 1946 at

performances—the only Porter musical ever to do so—and winning no less than five Tony awards. 1948 also saw the launch of composer Frank Loesser's first-ever Broadway show, *Where's Charley*. Originally a lyricist for Hoagy Carmichael, Jule Styne, and other major names, Loesser had begun writing music as well as words in the early 1940s, enjoying considerable success with his song *Praise the Lord and Pass the Ammunition,* and later winning an Oscar for another favorite number, *Baby It's Cold Outside,* featured in the 1949 Esther Williams movie, *Neptune's Daughter*. In November, 1950, Loesser's second musical, *Guys and Dolls*, was premiered at Broadway's 46th Street Theatre. The Damon Runyon-inspired show was his greatest achievement, running for 1,200 performances; a film version, starring Frank Sinatra and Marlon Brando, was released in 1955.

Below: Gene Kelly, Stanley Donen, and Leila Ernst appearing in a scene from Richard Rodgers and Lorenz Hart's Pal Joey on Broadway in 1940. The show received only lukewarm reviews, and closed the following year.

Left: An Indian dance sequence from Act I of Irving Berlin's Annie Get Your Gun, photographed on September 6, 1947 in performance at the Imperial Theatre, New York, where the show ran for a total of 1,147 performances.

Above: Artist Sam Warshaw, working from an earlier sketch, puts the finishing touches to a backdrop for the original Broadway production of Annie Get Your Gun in May, 1946. It features a picture of Buffalo Bill on horseback.

Broadway's Imperial Theatre. Like *Oklahoma!*, it had an undemanding but enjoyable storyline, and a homely, Western setting that inspired Berlin, a quintessential city boy from New York's Lower East Side, to create songs such as *Anything You Can Do (I Can Do Better), The Girl That I Marry,* and *There's No Business Like Show Business*, sung unforgettably by Ethel Merman in the original production.

Another outstanding postwar Broadway musical, *Kiss Me Kate*, was a subtle mix of drama, with Shakespeare's *The Taming of the Shrew* as a "play-within-a-play," dance, and sophisticated music and lyrics from the pen of Cole Porter. Starring Alfred Drake, Patricia Morison, and Lisa Kirk, it opened at the New Century Theatre in 1948, receiving over 1,000

Great Writers of the '40s

Inevitably, war left its mark on many American writers and their work during the decade. The debut novels by Gore Vidal and Norman Mailer, two of the most exciting new authors to emerge after 1945, drew directly on their experiences in the armed forces. Vidal's *Williwaw* (1946) was inspired by his service on an Army supply ship, while in *The Naked and the Dead* (1948), Mailer vividly conveyed the gruesome realities of jungle fighting in the South Pacific. The conflict proved to be less of an inspiration for Ernest Hemingway, whose classic, Spanish Civil War-based novel, *For Whom The Bell Tolls*, appeared in 1940; he spent most of 1942 and 1943 in Cuba, carrying out counter-espionage and submarine hunting operations, and published no other fiction during the decade. In contrast, William S. Burroughs, who made his debut with the notorious *Junkie* in 1953, took extreme measures to ensure his own unfitness for the draft by deliberately damaging his trigger finger!

No American writers of the 1940s were quite as shocking as Burroughs was later to be, but many readers and critics were scandalized by Vidal's 1948 novel, *The City and the Pillar*, which dealt openly with a homosexual relationship between its two main characters. Nevertheless, the book was warmly praised by the distinguished German author, Thomas Mann, then a U.S. resident, and the controversy surrounding it helped to boost its sales. Earlier, Mary McCarthy's first book, a semi-autobiographical collection of short stories titled *The Company She Keeps* (1942), had also created a considerable stir and widespread

Below: A promotional poster for the movie version of Raymond Chandler's 1943 novel The Lady In The Lake, *showing its stars Robert Montgomery (center—also the film's director), Audrey Totter, and Lloyd Nolan.*

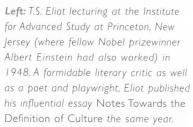

Left: T.S. Eliot lecturing at the Institute for Advanced Study at Princeton, New Jersey (where fellow Nobel prizewinner Albert Einstein had also worked) in 1948. A formidable literary critic as well as a poet and playwright, Eliot published his influential essay Notes Towards the Definition of Culture *the same year.*

acclaim. McCarthy's biting wit and sexually liberated attitudes had a particular impact on her younger peers; Norman Mailer described her as "our First Lady of letters" in Frances Kiernan's McCarthy biography, *Seeing Mary Plain*. Her later work included *The Groves of Academe* (1952) and *The Group* (1963).

One of the great earlier names in American literature, F. Scott Fitzgerald, author of *The Great Gatsby* and *Tender Is The Night*, died in 1940, but other established writers saw their reputations grow steadily during the decade. Poet and playwright T.S. Eliot (born in St. Louis, Missouri, but a U.K. citizen since 1927) issued his *Four Quartets* in 1943; five years later he was awarded both the British Order of Merit and the Nobel Prize for Literature. In 1949, the Nobel committee also honored William Faulkner, whose books in the 1940s included *Go Down, Moses* (1942) and *Intruder In The Dust* (1948). And in 1946, Raymond Chandler, creator of private detective Philip Marlowe (introduced six years earlier in Chandler's novel *The Big Sleep*) received the coveted Edgar Allen Poe Award from the Mystery Writers of America; he was to win it again in 1954.

American Classical Music

With the notable exception of Charles Ives (1874–1954), a rugged individualist whose powerful, sometimes startling music drew its inspiration exclusively from American life, landscape, and traditions, most pre-World War II U.S. classical composers wrote in a strongly European style. Given their training, this was almost inevitable; many promising young musicians were sent across the Atlantic (especially to Germany) to refine their skills, while those attending American colleges were largely taught by Old World émigrés whose cultural roots were still in their original homelands.

Ives was a role-model for younger U.S. composers seeking a more distinctive, "nationalist" voice, but his own works, often ferociously difficult to perform, were not widely heard for many years, and ill health drastically reduced his output in the last twenty-five years of his life. It took a younger man with a more populist approach, Aaron Copland (1900–1990), to attract substantial audiences to a new, clearly American type of classical music. Copland, born in New York but trained in Paris, enjoyed his first major success in the mid-1930s, after abandoning an earlier compositional style described by critic Harold C. Schonberg as "dissonant, percussive…abstract." Following the completion of *El salón México* in 1936, he embarked on what were to be among his most popular pieces—the three highly acclaimed ballet scores *Billy The Kid* (1938), *Rodeo* (1940), and *Appalachian Spring* (1944—awarded a Pulitzer Prize in 1945). These

Above: Martha Graham as The Bride in the original 1944 production of Copland's Appalachian Spring. *She also choreographed the ballet, which was dedicated to her.*

all feature brilliant scoring and prominent use of American folk melodies, the most famous of which is *Appalachian Spring*'s major theme, the old Shaker song, *Simple Gifts*.

The Musicians who fled Nazism

Among the other major figures emerging at the same time as Copland were several who, like him, had been students of composer, keyboardist, and conductor Nadia Boulanger (1887–1979) in France. This group, including Roy Harris, Virgil Thomson, and Elliot Carter, went on to play a significant part in U.S. music

Above: Oklahoma-born Roy Harris (1898–1979) later became Composer Laureate of the State of California, and also taught music at a number of major American universities, including Cornell, Princeton, and UCLA.

over the next few decades. However, their work, though popular, attracted a few dissenting voices. German émigré composer Arnold Schoenberg (see opposite) commented sourly in 1949 that " la Boulanger's pupils…have taken over American musical life, lock, stock, and barrel."

American orchestras—and the nation's entire cultural life—were greatly enriched by the influx of refugee musicians from Nazi Germany in the 1930s. After escaping from Berlin via Switzerland, the distinguished conductor Otto Klemperer became director of the Los Angeles Philharmonic in 1933, and subsequently appeared with the New York Philharmonic and other leading U.S. ensembles. His colleague, Bruno Walter, fled first Germany and then Austria before settling in America in 1939, and was appointed principal conductor of the NYPO eight years later. Several important German composers also succeeded in establishing themselves in the U.S.A. during the same period—among them Kurt Weill, of *Threepenny Opera* fame, and the father of serialism, Arnold Schoenberg.

The enforced move from Europe to America was not easy for these men. Though at the top of their profession, they often earned far less in the New World than they had commanded in their homelands, and some aspects of U.S. musical life were not to their taste. In Peter Heyworth's 1973 book *Conversations with Klemperer*, the conductor described his dislike for appearing at the Hollywood Bowl ("it's not very dignified"), and commented that, during his stay in the U.S., "I felt in the wrong place. The orchestras [on the East Coast] are good, technically. But one cannot compare them with, for instance, the Vienna Philharmonic." Klemperer eventually moved back to Switzerland, although other musical émigrés, including Walter, Weill, and Schoenberg, remained in America for the rest of their lives.

Below: *The great German conductor Bruno Walter (1876–1962) with the New York Philharmonic Orchestra in a scene from the film* Carnegie Hall, *released in 1947.*

A group of riders trekking along a path at the Grand Canyon in about 1950.

CHAPTER
EIGHT

LET'S GO!

Destination Unlimited

"On the first of May
It is moving day;
Spring is here, so blow your job,
Throw your job away;
Now's the time to trust
To your wanderlust.
In the city's dust you wait,
Must you wait? Just you wait:

"In a mountain greenery,
Where God paints the scenery,
Just two crazy people together;
While you love your lover, let
Blue skies be your coverlet,
When it rains we'll laugh at
the weather."

FROM MOUNTAIN GREENERY
BY LORENZ HART (1895–1943)

By 1940, transportation within the U.S.A. was more accessible and affordable than it had ever been before. Cars and gas were readily available, the highway network itself had undergone steady improvements since its reorganization fourteen years earlier (see pages 132–133), and Greyhound bus lines, founded in 1929, were already serving some 4,750 destinations. Meanwhile, railroads, though they were slowly declining in importance, still boasted some 230,000 miles of track, and airlines—the fastest growing of all passenger carriers—were reporting a 40 percent increase in traffic. Such developments had obvious benefits for business, and, later, for the nation's war effort. They also had a profound effect on the millions of individuals and families who could now afford to travel extensively for pleasure—and were able to see more of their country (and of the world beyond it) than any previous generation of Americans.

To take full advantage of this liberty, would-be holidaymakers needed adequate, paid vacation time—something which U.S. companies had been much slower to grant (especially to manual and industrial workers) than their European counterparts. Professor Cindy S. Aron's *Working At Play—A History of Vacations in the United States* quotes a survey, conducted in 1918 and 1919, which reveals that "while 85 percent [of 624 participating firms] gave their office workers paid vacations, only 18 percent furnished the same benefit to factory workers." Over the following years, this position gradually changed as more staff at all levels received holiday pay, though its provision was still far from universal two decades later.

Right: This group of late 1940s youth hostellers has just finished a cycling trip beside the Minnehaha Creek in Minneapolis. They are now posing for a photograph against the dramatic backdrop of Minnehaha Falls, close to where the creek enters the Mississippi River.

1940s TIMELINE

1940
TWA begins using the Boeing 307, the first pressurized passenger airplane, on its coast-to-coast U.S. routes.

1946
A consortium of ski enthusiasts and businessmen sets up the Aspen Ski Corporation to develop the city's winter sports facilities.

October 16, 1946
The Cunard liner *Queen Elizabeth*, completed in 1938, makes her maiden voyage from Southampton, England to New York.

April 24, 1950
The Desert Inn opens on The Strip in Las Vegas with a two-day gala including live entertainment from Edgar Bergen, bandleader Ray Noble, and other stars.

Without it, poorer employees were heavily restricted in their leisure options. Some of them could take advantage of subsidized or free accommodation in company-owned boarding houses at resorts near

Above: A huge crowd of vacationers enjoy sun, sea, and sand at Coney Island in 1945.

their workplaces, but the atmosphere in such places was often oppressive, with curfews, bans on alcohol, and other restrictions. The rules were even more draconian at the "vacation homes" run for young, single working-class women by churches and charities. A discontented resident of one of these institutions commented, in an article quoted by Professor Aron, that "'You can't even look at a man if you go there! I do not want to be bound to go to prayers twice a day.'" Properly funded vacations enabled employees to escape forever from this kind of paternalism, and do exactly what they wanted.

The rich, of course, had always enjoyed this freedom. Only the coming of war could restrict their opportunities, as most foreign holidays and cruises became temporarily impossible (though there was still some scope for luxurious vacationing within the U.S.A.). Nevertheless, the international air and shipping carriers continued to promote their services during the years of conflict, promising, in the words of an ad issued jointly by "The Airlines of the United States," "even faster and finer planes and…vastly extended operations…[when] the war is over." After 1945, they made good on this undertaking, expanding their range of routes, and also reducing their fares to attract a wider range of passengers. Despite these changes, however, the vast majority of U.S. vacationers in the 1940s still preferred to remain inside America's borders, and in the next few pages, we take a closer look at some of the destinations and types of travel they enjoyed during the pre- and postwar periods.

Above: A couple watch the clouds roll by from their rocktop vantage point in California's Angeles National Forest.

Favorite Destinations

In the 1940s, many Americans—like today's generation—spent their annual vacations relaxing at the beach or lakeside, taking the opportunity to catch the sun, enjoy some fishing, or play a little golf. Families might stay in a hotel or a boarding house, or even move into private lodgings for the season. In the introduction to Cindy S. Aron's history of U.S. vacations, the author recalls that "in 1944 my grandparents bought a summer house…on the Connecticut shore, [and] for years thereafter [our] entire extended family…fit, a little tightly, into the seven bedrooms. The women and children remained from mid June until Labor Day. The men came only for the weekends…[driving] down from the city on Friday nights." Other vacationers, taking shorter breaks, preferred to get as far away as possible from home and work, and increasing numbers of them began heading south or west to be sure of warmer weather. By the early 1940s, Florida and California were favorite (and still relatively uncommercialized) vacation destinations; Florida alone was welcoming over 2.5 million visitors a year at the start of the decade.

Travelers seeking more active, varied vacations were also well catered for, whether they were attracted to the great outdoors or the big cities. Most major National Parks were now easily accessible by road or rail. The Union Pacific provided transportation to Yellowstone and Utah's Bryce Canyon, while visitors to the Grand Canyon could take the main railroad line to Williams, Arizona and complete their journey via a special train. If they came by road to Williams on Route 66, they could also enjoy a side trip through the extraordinary Petrified Forest about 160 miles to the east.

Tourists bound for major urban centers were able to experience the speed and comfort of the diesel-powered rail services that had been slashing long-distance travel times since their introduction in the 1930s; by 1947, "The Golden Rocket" could cover the 2,500 miles from Chicago to Los Angeles via Minneapolis and El Paso in under 40 hours. Equipped with sleeping and dining cars, these trains were as luxurious as many hotels, ensuring that passengers were ready for the rigors of sightseeing or shopping as soon as they reached their destinations.

Below: The Will Rogers Hotel, in Claremore, OK, offered guests "Western welcome and Southern hospitality."

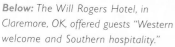

Right: The Boston & Maine Railroad's "Minute Man" express, seen just beyond Yoar Curve, Deerfield, Massachusetts, in August, 1944.

Some wartime vacationers had more pressing, personal reasons for their trips. While sailors were on shore leave, their wives or girlfriends often visited naval ports to snatch a few precious days with them, and thousands of couples were reunited on the pier when the fleet came home for good in 1945. In a touching scene from the first of Armistead Maupin's *Tales of the City* novels, the mother of one character recalls how, after V-J Day, her sailor husband took her to San Francisco's nineteenth floor Top of the Mark "sky lounge" on the city's Nob Hill, with its spectacular view over the bay where his ship was anchored. "I remember he slipped the bandleader five dollars, so we could dance to 'Moonlight Serenade,' and I spilled [my] Tom Collins all over his beautiful white Navy [uniform]…"

Most of the locations mentioned above are perennial vacation favorites, enjoyed by generations of Americans. However, the decade also saw the emergence of some new leisure activities, catering for a wide—and often sharply contrasting—range of clienteles. Two of these are featured overleaf.

Left and below right: The Chicago-Seattle-Tacoma "Hiawatha" train, with its streamlined rolling stock and luxurious observation cars, seen in 1948. It was operated by the "Milwaukee Road" (Chicago, Milwaukee, St. Paul, and Pacific Railroad).

Below left: An ad for "The Exposition Flyer," the high-speed Chicago-San Francisco passenger service launched in 1939 by the Chicago, Burlington, & Quincy Railroad.

Skiing and Gambling

Winter sports and casino gambling are now multi-million dollar businesses; the 1940s saw each of these once low-profile (and, in the case of gambling, widely illegal) pastimes attain greater popularity, and begin to assume their modern, highly commercialized forms.

Information published by the Aspen Historical Society shows that as early as the 1860s, skiing was both a hobby and a convenient means of transportation for silver miners and local residents in the Colorado Rockies. A decade later, skis (or snowshoes) were in recreational use in Southern California, and by the 1900s, the sport was well-established in New England and Michigan. Over the following years, skiing clubs sprang up in other suitable locations, such as Lake Placid in New York State, site of the third Winter Olympics in 1932, and soon, far-sighted entrepreneurs were starting to develop luxurious resorts for the sport's often wealthy devotees. Union Pacific Railroad chairman, Averill Harriman, backed the successful Sun Valley complex near Ketchum, Idaho, which opened in 1936. The same year, Billy Fiske, T.J. Flynn, and Ted Ryan launched the Highland Bavarian Lodge in Aspen, Colorado, whose top-class accommodation and spectacular ski runs were designed to match (or exceed) anything its well-heeled customers could expect to find in the European Alps.

As the political situation in Germany and Austria worsened, a number of prominent skiing experts from those countries fled to America; during World War II, some of them served alongside their U.S.-born counterparts in the Tenth Mountain Division of ski-borne troops, stationed at Camp Hale, about thirty-five miles east of Aspen. After the war, the Aspen area remained a major center for winter sports, and soon, massive investment and impressive new facilities were reshaping it as, in the words of one headline, a "World Ski Capital." Nevertheless, rival resorts, in Southern California and elsewhere, also had much to offer, and were soon attracting new visitors of their own. By the end of the decade, skiers with a musical bent could even book themselves a vacation at a mountain lodge in Stowe, Vermont run by the

Right: Punters at Harold's Club, Reno, Nevada. Reno, like Las Vegas (John Gunther's Inside U.S.A. described their relationship as being similar to that of San Francisco and Los Angeles), was already a thriving gaming center in the 1940s, and Harold's was its biggest casino.

Above and left: Railroad travelers en route for skiing vacations in New Hampshire, Vermont, and Canada could check this information board, seen at Boston's North Station in 1946, to ensure that snow conditions would be as perfect as those on the magazine cover!

The Flamingo's flash opulence, partly inspired by clubs that Siegel had previously owned in Los Angeles, set the tone for future Las Vegas "resorts," and made The Strip the hottest location for them. A fourth hotel, The Thunderbird, opened there in 1948, and 1950 saw the launch of Wilbur Clark's 300-room Desert Inn—the biggest of all the early Strip properties, with its own golf course, a 2,400 square-foot casino, and a host of other impressive amenities. The DI was a huge success—according to Las Vegas historian, Deanna DeMatteo, its profits after just a week of trading were a staggering $750,000—and, as other resort owners devised their own strategies to entice both high-rollers and small-time gamblers through their doors, the modern Las Vegas was born.

Above: *Two couples enjoying a night out on Main Street in Las Vegas in March, 1940. During this period, Vegas's downtown area, with its then restrained decor and illuminations, was the city's gaming center; the first casino on The Strip (which lies beside the highway to Los Angeles), El Rancho, did not open until the following year.*

Von Trapp family, who were soon to be immortalized in Rodgers and Hammerstein's *The Sound of Music!*

Las Vegas, Nevada has none of the natural beauty of the Rockies; in the early 1930s, it was, in the words of British-born journalist Alistair Cooke, just "a dusty Western town…whose water came from an Artesian well, whose chamber of commerce was a one-story stuccoed building, whose baseball park seated seven hundred, whose cottonwoods still shaded the relics of its old Mormon stockade." A little later, thanks to hydroelectric power from the newly built Hoover Dam, the city gradually began to expand. But it was Nevada's liberal gaming laws (it had legalized casino gambling in 1931, and was the only state to permit it during the 1940s), and the arrival of men determined to take advantage of them, that truly transformed its fortunes.

For mobster Benjamin "Bugsy" Siegel, a man already active in illicit gambling, Las Vegas was a haven from which he could operate openly. After several years of involvement in downtown clubs there, he became attracted to a less-developed highway-side area soon to become known as The Strip. In the early 1940s, it boasted just two major hotels, the El Rancho Vegas and the Last Frontier. After the war, Siegel acquired a controlling interest in an unfinished third property, subsequently named the Flamingo, and went on to supervise its completion (with the aid of underworld cash) and run it until his assassination in 1947.

Greyhound Buses
and the Photography of Esther Bubley

The Greyhound bus line began as a tiny, Minnesota-based transportation firm in 1914. By 1922, it had merged with a group of other Midwestern carriers to form the Motor Transit Corporation. After a series of further expansions, a new long-distance service provider, Northbound Transportation Corporation, was born four years later. This company used the Greyhound name, and introduced the famous "running dog" logo that has graced its vehicles ever since; it was officially rechristened Greyhound Corporation in 1930.

As inexpensive, readily accessible alternatives to the railroad, Greyhounds quickly became an American institution, attracting millions of passengers every year, and even finding their way into movies, song lyrics, and poetry. However, the actual experience of traveling long distances in the firm's early, wood-bodied vehicles could be highly uncomfortable, especially during the winter, and passengers eagerly welcomed the advent of air-conditioned Greyhound "Super-Coaches" in 1936. A few years later, these models started to sport the distinctive metal side-trim that was soon to become another company trademark.

At the start of the 1940s, Greyhound's extensive advertising campaigns often linked bus journeys to fun and leisure, but the coming of World War II brought an inevitable change in emphasis. One memorable ad from 1941 featured a map of the nation's principal defense centers, and offered information on how to reach them. Later campaigns warned against unnecessary travel, showed buses filled with homecoming servicemen ("Another great job for the bus lines...the one we like the best"), and announced, with justifiable pride, that Greyhounds had carried nearly 3 billion passengers in the period from Pearl Harbor to 1945. Peacetime saw the return of colorful inducements to would-be vacationers, who were reminded that Greyhound served all forty-eight states (as well as Canada and Mexico), and gave its customers "first choice in comfort, convenience, and economy."

These ads, with their glamorous, idealized illustrations, are fascinating, but the starker, black-and-white photos shot in buses and depots (shown on these pages) by Esther Bubley (1921–1998) convey a far truer, more evocative sense of Greyhound travel during the decade. Bubley, hired as a technician at the Office of War Information in early 1943, quickly persuaded her boss, Roy Stryker, to use her as a photographer there, and her first major assignment, a series of vivid, characterful pictures of Greyhound passengers, taken on a return trip from Washington D.C. to Memphis that September, demonstrates an extraordinary empathy with her subjects. As Bubley commented in a later interview, "Put me down with people, and it's just incredible."

On the Road

In 1926, the U.S. highway network, whose haphazard organization and poor state of repair had been a serious obstacle to the growth of motoring, was radically restructured. Major routes were given numbers, systematic signposting was introduced, and federal funding was provided for maintenance and new construction. Over the following years, thousands of miles of dirt- and gravel-surfaced roads were paved (this work provided a significant source of employment during the Depression), and by 1940, many of America's nearly 32.5 million car owners were becoming accustomed to driving long distances for business and leisure.

Below: A wall map showing the most celebrated of the newly numbered roads introduced in 1926—Route 66, which passes through eight states on its way to Los Angeles.

Above: This 1941 Oldsmobile Series 60 five-passenger sedan had all the power and comfort needed for long-distance travel on America's rapidly improving roads, though its use on wartime journeys would have been severely restricted by gas rationing.

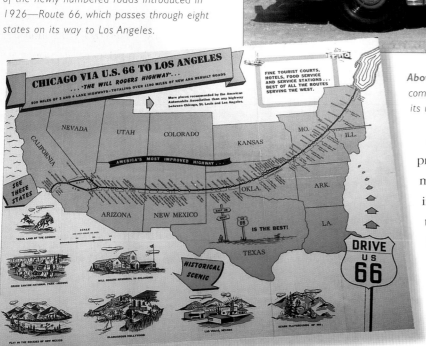

As traffic increased, more and more roadside businesses sprang up to provide these travelers with food, gas, and accommodation. During the mid-1920s, the proprietor of an inn at San Luis Obispo, California invented the word "motel" (motor hotel) to describe his premises, but the term was not widely adopted until much later. Most highway lodgings in the 1940s were known as "motor courts" or "tourist courts"; they housed their guests in individual cabins or chalets, and offered basic, but usually clean and comfortable accommodation. Decor and amenities varied relatively little, though there were some

Above: *A rare two-door prototype version of Chrysler's Town and Country hardtop coupe, built in 1946. Only seven of these cars were made in that year; the company's sales team felt that the design was unlikely to sell, and quickly reverted to the four-door model.*

more novel and even bizarre motor courts, like the "wigwam villages" dreamed up by Kentucky entrepreneur, Frank A. Redford, in which tourists stayed in concrete teepees! Redford's concept spread to several other states, and three wigwam-style motels (in Cave City, Kentucky, Holbrook, Arizona, and Rialto, California) still survive today.

The outbreak of war led to a temporary decline in automobile ownership, as production of civilian vehicles ceased, and fuel rationing sharply restricted non-essential journeys. However, sales rose quickly again after 1945, and postwar buyers soon had an impressive range of models to choose from, including new versions of Chrysler's wooden-sided Town and Country, the first Cadillacs with tail fins (introduced in 1948), and other outstanding designs from Studebaker, Packard ("America's Number 1 Glamour Car") and Pontiac. The man who had done more than any other manufacturer to popularize motoring, Henry Ford, died on April 7, 1947, at the age of eighty-three, but his company—and the rest of the car industry—continued to flourish. By 1950, the U.S.A. was making two-thirds of the world's automobiles, and over 49 million had been sold.

Harley-Davidson— King of the Road

Before the onset of the Depression, demand among sportsmen and regular riders for high-performance motorcycles had kept a number of specialist manufacturers, both large and small, in business. Sadly, almost all of these firms were wiped out in the 1930s, and for the next two decades, the only major American bike makers were Harley-Davidson of Milwaukee, Wisconsin, and its Springfield, Massachusetts-based arch-rival Indian, which had been formed within a year of each other at the start of the century.

Initially, Indian was the larger of the two; by 1914, it had become the biggest producer of motorcycles in the world. However, after World War I (during which both companies supplied thousands of machines to the military), its manufacturing totals fell behind Harley-Davidson's, and it began to suffer from management problems, although the technical excellence of its designs remained a serious challenge to its main competitor. Meanwhile, Harley went from strength to strength—until the calamitous events of 1929 and their aftermath, which (like Indian) it barely survived.

Harley-Davidson restored its fortunes in 1936 with the EL "Knucklehead," featuring a 61ci/1000cc, overhead valve "big twin" engine with the bulging rocker boxes that gave it its

Above: *H-D were reaching out to a new market with the cozy image on this 1940s catalog.*

nickname. Priced at $380, it sold well, and was followed by a string of other popular models—including a new, 74ci/1200cc Knucklehead, the FL74, which debuted in 1941. With the outbreak of World War II, Harley and Indian discontinued civilian bike production, but many of the servicemen who rode the special "Army-version" motorcycles made by the two companies between 1942 and 1945 became eager customers for their postwar machines. Among these was Harley's 1948 overhead valve "Panhead," the forerunner of the "hogs" used by Peter Fonda and Dennis Hopper in the 1969 movie *Easy Rider.* In 1945, Indian introduced a new version of its classic Chief (whose first incarnation had appeared in 1922), but the firm's attempts to launch

a range of lighter bikes proved unsuccessful, and contributed to its eventual closure in 1953—leaving Harley-Davidson, which celebrated its fiftieth anniversary the same year, as American's sole motorcycle manufacturer.

Left: *Another publicity shot seeking to promote the idea of Harley-Davidsons as a suitable alternative to a small car for fun-loving young couples.*

Taking Flight

The classic 1933 Fred Astaire and Ginger Rogers movie *Flying Down to Rio*, with its memorable title song and brilliantly choreographed, airplane-inspired final dance sequence, captures the excitement and exoticism once synonymous with taking to the skies. Even during the Depression years, well-heeled vacationers could wing their way to a wide range of destinations in Brazil, Mexico, or the Caribbean. By the end of the decade, journeys to more distant locations were in prospect, as Pan American flying boats pioneered transpacific services to the Philippines (in 1936) before inaugurating regular Atlantic crossings, via New Brunswick, the Azores, and Portugal, three years later.

The elegance and comfort provided by these airlines were in sharp contrast to the spartan conditions endured by earlier flyers. Charles E. Levine, the first-ever transatlantic plane passenger, had to sit on an oil drum throughout his forty-two-hour trip from America to Germany with pilot Clarence Duncan Chamberlin in June, 1927

Above: Personal service…a Pennsylvania-Central Airlines porter carries passengers' luggage from plane to terminal building after a 1945 flight. PCA was renamed Central in 1948.

Right: A United Airlines Douglas DC-3, City of Portland, *about to leave the runway. United acquired their first DC-3s in 1936, the year after the airplane's introduction. Though the model ceased production in 1946, over 1,000 DC-3s still remain in service around the world.*

(made less than a month after Charles Lindbergh's historic solo flight to Paris). Little more than a decade later, customers on state-of-the-art craft, like the Boeing B-314 "clippers" used by PanAm, were relaxing in elegantly appointed interiors and enjoying their meals in specially designed on-board dining rooms. Shorter-haul airplanes of the period, such as the Douglas DC-3 and Boeing Stratoliner, also offered broad, spacious cabins, frequently fitted out with sleeping berths, lounges, and other amenities, as well as impressive performance statistics—the DC-3 could cross America in just eighteen hours.

During the 1940s, the airlines' promise of speed combined with luxury enabled them to poach customers from their arch-rivals, the shipping lines and railroads. Many vacationers still preferred the gentle joys of a sea-cruise to Hawaii or Acapulco to the unfamiliar—and occasionally unnerving—experience of flying. Cunard, whose ships, *Queen Mary* and *Queen Elizabeth*, took just five days to steam from Southampton, England to New York, remained, for the present, the major transatlantic carrier. But for business executives and other travelers in a hurry, planes were growing steadily in importance, and, after the war, increasing numbers of affluent, adventurous Americans began using them to see more of the world.

The great attraction of flying was the fact that, in the words of one 1940s ad, "its tremendous velocity creates the time for travel." When going by sea, a substantial part of a vacation might be used up in reaching and returning from a distant country, but by air, thanks to a postwar generation of planes capable of lengthy non-stop flights, no more than two days were usually needed for outward and return journeys. The introduction of an overnight sleeper service to Europe by TWA in October, 1948 gave passengers even more precious daylight time at their destinations—though,

Above: Travelers relax in the spacious, pleasantly appointed cabin of a TWA airliner in the mid-1940s.

as airplane parts supplier AirLiance comments on its website, the combination of noisy piston engines and low-altitude turbulence (propeller-powered planes rarely exceeded cruising heights of 18,000 feet) probably kept most of them awake during the flight!

By 1949, the number of passengers carried by America's commercial airlines had exceeded 16 million, and the world's first jet airliner—the British-designed Comet—was already in service. Nevertheless, civil aviation in America (as in Europe and elsewhere) remained sheltered from the full impact of market forces. Companies were forbidden, by the U.S. Civil Aeronautics Board, from trying to undercut their rivals, and ticket

prices on domestic and international routes were relatively high, though there had been reductions since 1945, and some "coach class" fares were beginning to appear. However, the advent of stiffer competition would soon lead to further expansion, and before many more years had passed, American travelers would be looking beyond the prospect of *Flying Down to Rio*, and aspiring to the wider vistas of Sammy Cahn and Jimmy Van Heusen's hymn to the long-haul, *Come Fly With Me*—the song immortalized in 1958 by Frank Sinatra, and conjuring up the prospect of an airborne romance whose pleasures are almost as enticing as the far-flung places to which the lovers in the song are headed.

How They Saw the Future

Science, Technology, and Transportation

"Nobody who is anybody a hundred years hence but will have his automobile and his air yacht."

"THINGS WILL BE SO DIFFERENT 100 YEARS HENCE,"
THE BROOKLYN DAILY EAGLE, DECEMBER 30, 1899

"Joseph J. O'Connell Jr., Chairman of the Civil Aeronautics Board, said that within three decades all the major cities of the world would be linked by jet transport aircraft with a normal cruising speed of at least six hundred miles an hour! 'In thirty years,' he went on, 'we should be able to have a great deal of our local passenger air service, and, within cities, connecting service, performed by helicopters.'

"Charles Sawyer, Secretary of Commerce, predicted that turbine-powered air transports flying at more than twice the speed of present-day commercial planes would provide a medium for mass travel.

"The size of airlines of the future will be governed more by economic factors than technical considerations, according to Dr. Edward Warner, president of the Council of the International Civil Aviation Organization. Within a few years, he said, there will be nothing to prevent a five-hundred-passenger plane being built but there will be no economic advantage to constructing one."

THE NEW YORK TIMES REPORT ON A FORTHCOMING
U.N. RADIO BROADCAST DEVOTED TO THE INTERNATIONAL
CIVIL AVIATION ORGANIZATION, APRIL 23, 1950

The designers of all types of transportation know the many advantages of light alloys as engineered and produced by Bohn.

Above: *One of a series of ads produced by the Bohn Aluminum and Brass Corporation of Detroit during the last few months of the war. Their images and copywriting often combined wide-ranging (and sometimes outlandish) speculations about future technologies with vigorous promotion of the company's engineering capabilities, and of the part it planned to play in shaping the postwar world.*

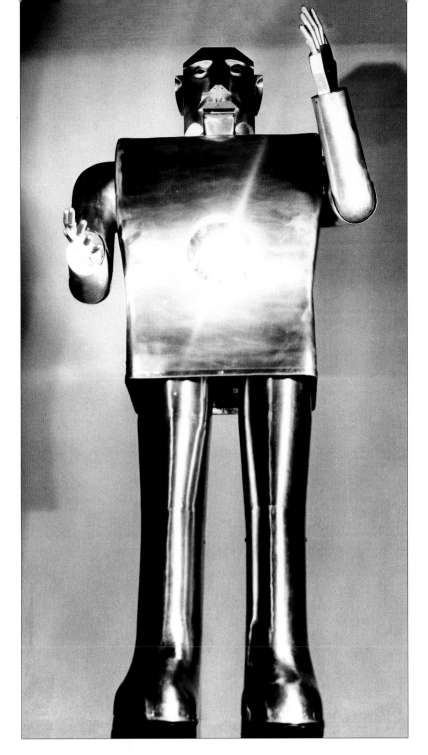

"For mature thought there is no mechanical substitute. But creative thought and essentially repetitive thought are very different things. For the latter there are, and may be, powerful mechanical aids. [...] "The world has arrived at an age of cheap complex devices of great reliability; and something is bound to come of it."

DR. VANNEVAR BUSH, DIRECTOR OF OFFICE OF SCIENTIFIC RESEARCH AND DEVELOPMENT, "AS WE MAY THINK," ATLANTIC MONTHLY, JULY, 1945

"It is hardly necessary to inform you that life in those times will be as nearly a holiday as it is possible to make it. Work will be reduced to a minimum by machinery."

THE BROOKLYN DAILY EAGLE, DECEMBER 30, 1899

"For those who like to take their ocean voyages at high speed but do not wish to relinquish such luxuries as swimming pools, orchestras, and sun decks, etc., [...] why not [create] giant, jet-propelled ships which could provide the desired comforts and at the same time have the faster speed?

AD FOR BOHN ALUMINUM & BRASS CORPORATION, WHEN DREAM SHIPS COME TRUE, 1945

"To primitive man, his ten fingers and ten toes were natural computing devices. In a later age, piles of pebbles were the accepted mathematical aids. [...] But for modern man, there must be gigantic mechanical robots, capable of speedy and precise analysis of complicated problems."

NEWSWEEK, OPENING TO A REPORT ON THE ENIAC COMPUTER, FEBRUARY 18, 1946

"I think there is a world market for maybe five computers."

THOMAS WATSON, CHAIRMAN OF IBM, 1943

How They Saw the Future

Freedom, Prosperity, and Security

"Freedom is an indivisible word. If we want to enjoy it, we must be prepared to extend it to everyone, whether they are rich or poor, whether they agree with us or not, no matter what their race or the color of their skin. We cannot, with good conscience, expect the British to set up an orderly schedule for the liberation of India before we have decided for ourselves to make all who live in America free."

WENDELL WILLKIE, *ONE WORLD*, 1943

"Nothing, perhaps, has altered the world more in all the history of Western civilization than rising American productivity has in the last half century. And barring atomic annihilation, nothing is more likely to alter the world so much in the next half century." *FORTUNE* MAGAZINE, COMMENTING ON THE SUCCESS OF POSTWAR U.S. BUSINESS, JULY, 1955

"It is an unfortunate fact…that the peace we hoped for has not come quickly. We are still living in hazardous times. We are required to give unremitting thought to the defense of the United States at a period when defense has become incredibly more difficult. American scientists must, like all the rest of our citizens, devote a part of their strength and skill to keeping the Nation strong. At a time when we hoped our scientific efforts could be directed almost exclusively to improving the well-being of our people we must, instead, make unprecedented peacetime efforts to maintain our military strength. For we have learned the hard and bitter way that we cannot hope for lasting peace with justice if we do not remain strong in the cause of peace." PRESIDENT HARRY S. TRUMAN, ADDRESSING THE AMERICAN ASSOCIATION FOR THE ADVANCEMENT OF SCIENCE AT ITS CENTENNIAL MEETING IN WASHINGTON D.C., SEPTEMBER, 1948

"America was thus clearly top nation, and History came to a ."

W.C. SELLAR & R.J. YEATMAN, *1066 AND ALL THAT*, 1930

Opposite right: A new life in the New World in a new decade—an immigrant family gaze at the Statue of Liberty as they arrive in America in 1949.

Index

A & P 32, *32, 33*, 36, 42
Abbott, Bud 80–1, *80*, 98
Acheson, Dean 21
advertising 89, 93
airplanes 127, 136–7, 138
Allen, Fred 89, *89*
Allen, Gracie *79*
American Community Builders 47
American Gas Corporation 54
Amos 'n' Andy 80, *80–1*, 89
Andrew Sisters *82–3*, 98
Anheuser-Busch 35
Armstrong company 52
Aron, Cindy S. 126, 127, 128
artists 117
Atlantic Charter 20
Auden, W.H. 116

Bacall, Lauren 100, *100*
Ball, Lucille *84*
barbecues 60, *60–1*
Bardeen, John 75
baseball 104, 106–7
Basie, Bill 83, *83*
bathrooms 56–7
Baudot, François 39
bedrooms 58–9
Beemer, Brace *85*
beer 35
Belmont radio 79
Benny, Jack 80, *81*, 99
Benson, Dr Allen H. 96–7
Bergen, Edgar *80–1*, 81
Bergman, Ingrid *98*, 99
Berle, Milton *81*, 90, *91*
Berlin, Irving 118–19
Bernstein, Joel 118
Bernstein, Leonard 116, 118, *118*
Beschloss, Michael 22
Birdseye, Clarence 31
Birkby, Evelyn & Bob 66

Blitz *12*, 13
Block, Martin 82
board games 61
Boddy, Chet 47
Bogart, Humphrey *98*, 99, 100
Boller, Carl & Robert 40, *41*
Borglum, Lincoln & Gutzon 117
Boulanger, Nadia 123
bowling 108–9
boxing 105, *105*
Brattain, Walter 75
Britten, Benjamin 116
Broadway 116, 118–19
Brochert, John R. 58–9
Brokaw, Tom 23
Brown, Warren 106
Brunot, James 61
Bubley, Esther 132
Burns, George 79
Burroughs, William S. 120
Butts, Alfred Mosher 61
Buxton, Frank 87

Caesar, Sid 92, *93*
calculating machines 73, *73*
cameras 75, *75*
Campbell, Thomas C. 66
Caniff, Milton 84
Carlson, Chester 73
Carnegie, Hattie 103
cars 41, 42, 134–5
Casablanca 40, 97, *98*, 99
chain broadcasting 78
chair design 52, *53*
Chambers, Whittaker 27
Chandler, Raymond 121
Cheney, Joyce 53
Chun, Ellery J. 24
churches 96–7
Churchill, Winston 20, *20*
clothing stores 39
coal strike 64–5, *64–5*
Coca, Imogene 92, *93*

Collier, John Jr. 58
Collyer, Bud 84
Columbia 52
comedy 80–1
Communism 26–7
computers 73, 74, *74*, 75, 139
Cooke, Alistair 39, 98, 131
Copland, Aaron 122–3
Correll, Charles 80, *80–1*
Costello, Lou 80–1, *80*, 98
Coughlin, Charles E. 13
Count Basie Orchestra 83, *83*
Crocker, Betty 55, *55*
Crosby, Bing 24
Cross, Robin 98
Cullen, Michael J. 36
Curtiss-Wright 69

Davis, Bette 98
Davis, Howard L. 93
Day, Ned *104*, 108
De Havilland, Olivia 101
decentralization 42–3
Deere, John *66*
DeMatteo, Deanna 131
Depression 40, 46, 134
Dies, Martin 27
DiMaggio, Joe *106*, 106, 107
Dior, Christian *102*, 103, *103*
"disc jockeys" 82
drama 84–5
drive-in theaters *40*, 41

Eames, Charles & Ray 52, *53*
Economic Cooperation Act 21
Edwards, Douglas 92
Eliot, T.S. *120*, 121
employment 16–17, 64–70, 72–3, 126
Employment Act 1946 64
ENIAC 65, 69, *74*, 75, 139

entertainment 76–93
Equal Pay Act 1963 69
Executive Orders 26, 27

Famous Door Club 83, *83*
farm life 66–7
fashion 31, 39, 102–3
fast food 34, 43
Federal Home Loan Bank Act 46
Federal Housing Administration (F.H.A.) 46, 47, 50
Federal National Mortgage Association 47
"Felix the Cat" *78*, 79
Fender, Clarence Leo 74, 75
Fibber McGee and Molly 80
Fisher, Irving 73
Fiske, Billy 130
Fitzgerald, F. Scott 121
Flynn, T.J. 130
Fogelson, Robert M. 42
food 34–7, 43, 55
football 104, 105
franchising 34
Freiberger, Paul 75
Furness, Betty 93

gambling 130–1
games 61
gardens 60–1
Garland, Judy *88*, 98, 100, *100*
gas power 54
Gehrig, Lou 106
"General Limitation Order" 39
Gershwin, George 118
"GI Bill of Rights" 21, 22–3, 22, 47, 50, 70
Gibson, John 22
Gibson, Walter B. 85
Gilman, George F. 32

Ginsberg, Allen 36
Goldman, Sylvan 36
golf 108
Gone With The Wind 98, 99, 101
Goodwin, Danny 89
Gosden, Freeman 80, *80–1*
Grabowicz, Paul 101
Graser, Earle 84
The Green Hornet 84
Grennard, Elliot 96
Greyhound buses 126, 132–3
Guest, Edgar A. 46
Gunther, John 27, 31, 48–9, 66, 70

Haley, Bill 113
Halgrimson, Andrea 32
Halnon, Mary 41
Halpert, Sam 17
Hammerstein, Oscar II 116, 117, 118, 131
Harding, Warren 86
Hardy, Rob 104–5
Harley-Davidson 135
Harriman, Averill 130
Harris, Roy 123, *123*
Harrison, Cynthia 69
Harrison, Wallace K. 21
Hart, Larry 118
Hart, Lorenz 126
Hartford, George H. 32
Hartley, Fred 65
Haswell, Oscar 108
Hawaii 24–5
Hearst, William Randolph 99
Heinz 55, *55*
Hemingway, Ernest 120, *121*
Hepburn, Katharine 16
Here's Morgan 81
Herman, Billy 106
Herrick, Elinore M. 69
Hester, Aline 65

Hewlett, Bill 74
Hewlett-Packard 74
Heyworth, Peter 123
Hiroshima 17
Hiss, Alger 27, *27*
Hitchcock, Alfred 100
Hollingshead, Richard M. Jr. 41
"Hollywood Ten" 27, 101
Home Owners Refinancing Act 46
Honig, Donald 106
Hoopii, Sol 24
Hoover, Herbert 46
Hope, Bob 80, *81*, *88*, 89, 91
horse racing 104–5
House Un-American Activities Committee (H.U.A.C.) 21, 27, 101
housing 44–61
Housing Act 1949 47
Howdy Doody 93, *93*

I Love A Mystery 85
Indian Claims Commission 26, *26*
Ives, Charles 122

Jackson, Kenneth 42
James, Richard 61
Japanese internment 23, *23*
"Jim Crow" laws 26
Johnson, Howard 34, 43
Jordan, Jim & Marian 80
Jordan, Louis 96, 97, *112*, 113

Kaiser, Henry J. 16
Kallman, Chester 116
Kaltenborn, H.V. 86–7
Kanter, Rosabeth Moss 72
Karney, Robyn 98
Kelly, Gene 101, *101*, *119*
Kemp, Tom 65
Kennedy, David M. 13, 47

Kenrick, John 118
Kern, Jerome 118
kitchens 54–5
Klemperer, Otto 123
Knox, Frank 14
Kotkin, Joel 101
Kroc, Ray 43
Kyser, Kay 82, *83*

Labor-Management Relations Bill 65
Land, Edwin Herbert 75
League of Nations 20
Lehman, Herbert H. 13
"Lend-Lease" Bill 14
Levine, Charles E. 136
Levitt, William & Alfred 47, 49, 50–1
Levittown 47, 50–60
Lewis, John L. *64*, 65
Lewis, Sinclair 30–1, 58
Liquid Paper 73
living rooms 52–3
Loesser, Frank 119
Loewy, Raymond 58
Lombard, Carole 99
The Lone Ranger 84, *85*, 91
Lopez, Juan Antonio 58, *58–9*
Louis, Joe 105, *105*
Lubitsch, Ernst 99
Lyons, Ted 106

McAndless, M. Thelma 70
MacArthur, General Douglas 20
McCardell, Claire *102*, 103
McCarthy, Mary 120–1
McDonald's 31, 43
McIntire, Lani 24
Mack, Ted 90–1
McLeod, Elizabeth 81
Magnavox 52
Mailer, Norman 120, 121
Main Streets 28–43
Malone, Bill C. 96
Manhattan Project 17, 69
Mann, Thomas 120
Marshall, George C. 21
Marshall Plan 21, 27
Maryland housing development *47*, 53
Matson Line 25, *25*

Maupin, Armistead 129
Meet The Press 92, *92*
microwave ovens 54
Miller, Arthur 117
Minnelli, Vincente 100
Mitchell, Margaret *99*
Monteux, Pierre 82
Moore, Arthur *11*
Morgan, Henry 81
Morgan, Irene 26
Morrison, Bret 85
Morse, Carlton E. 85, 91
mortgages 46, 47, 50
motels 134
Motion Picture Alliance for the Preservation of American Ideals 101
motorcycles 135
movies 31, 40–1, 98–101
Murrow, Edward R. 13, 79, 86, *86*
music 82–3, 96, 110, 112–13, 122–3
musicals 116, 118–19

Nagasaki *16*, 17
National Association for the Advancement of Colored People 26, *26*
National Broadcasting Company (NBC) 78, 79, 80–1
National Football League 104
National Parks 128
Nesmith Graham, Bette 73
Neutrality Acts 13
New Deal era 46–7
news 86–7, 92
Nolte, Frank G. 23
Norell, Norman 103
North Atlantic Treaty Organization (NATO) 21
nuclear bombs *16*, 17

O'Connell, Joseph J. Jr. 138
One Man's Family 85, 91
O'Neill, Eugene 117
Oppenheimer, Robert J. 17
The Original Amateur

Hour 90–1
Osborne, Beverly & Rubye 34, *34*
Owen, Bill 87
Owens, Josie Lucilla *17*
Oxley, Ethel *31*

Packard, Dave 74
Palladino, Grace 110
Park Forest 47, 51
Parkinson, David 100
Parnell Thomas, John 21
Patterson, James T. 64
Pearl Harbour 14, 24–5
Penney, James Cash 39
Penney stores *38*, 39, 42
Pepsodent toothpaste 89
Perelman, S.J. 48
phonographs 52
photocopiers 73
Piggly Wiggly store 36
Podell, Janet 97
Polaroid 75, *75*
Pons, Lily *88*
Porter, Cole 119
Post, Emily 72
Pratt, Anthony 61
Press-Radio War 86
Prohibition end 35

racism 16, 22–3, 26, 47, 51, 107, 108
radio 78–89, 113
railroads 126, 128, *128*, *129*
Randall, Gregory C. 49
Rankin, John E. 27
rationing 14, *15*, 31, 34, 35
RCA 52
Reagan, Ronald 55
records 52
Redford, Frank A. 135
refrigerators 54
restaurants 34, 43
roads 134–5
Robinson, Jackie 97, 107, *107*
Robinson, Sugar Ray 105
Robinson-Patman Act 32
Rockefeller, John D. Jr. 21
Rockwell, Norman *14*
Rodgers, Richard 116, 117, 118, 131

Rooney, Mickey 98
Roosevelt, Eleanor 13, 16, 59
Roosevelt, Franklin D. 13, *13*, 14, *20*
baseball 106
death 21, *21*
GI Bill 22
housing 46
Inaugural Address 21
United Nations 20
"Rosie the Riveter" campaign 16
Rushmore, Mount 117, *117*
Russell, Jane *83*, 103
Ruth, George Herman "Babe" 106
Ryan, Ted 130

Safeway 36, *36*
St. Paul's Cathedral *12*
Sakarin, Georgi 21
Sale, Charles "Chic" 56, *56*
Saunders, Clarence 36
Schlitz 35
Schoenberg, Arnold 123
Schonberg, Harold C. 122
schools 70–1
Schwartz Cowan, Ruth 56
Sears *38*, 39
Selective Service Act 69
Sellar, W.C. 140
The Shadow 85, *85*
Shelley family 47
Shirer, William L. 86
Shockley, William 75
Siegel, Benjamin "Bugsy" 131
Simmons company 59
Simon, George T. 82
Sinatra, Frank 24, *25*, 97, 101, *101*, 110, 112, 113, 119, 137
Skelton, Red *80*, 81
skiing 127, 130
Slinky 61, *61*
Smith, "Buffalo Bob" 93, *93*
Smith, Kate 80
Spivak, Charlie *83*
Spivak, Lawrence 92
sport 70, 86–7, 90, 104–9

Stalin, Josef 20, *20*, 66
Steinbeck, John 67
Stern, Bill 87, *87*
Stevenson, Robert Louis 24
Stokowski, Leopold 82, 117, *117*
Stravinsky, Igor 116
strikes 64–5
Sullivan, Ed 79
Superman 84
supermarkets 36–7
Swaine, Michael 75
Swayze, John Cameron 93

Tabor, Betty 34
Taft, Robert 65
Taylor, Elizabeth 100, *100*
"Teen-Age" 110–11
telegraph 73
television 52, 79, 90–3
tennis 105
Terry and the Pirates 84
Texaco 89
Texaco Star Theater 89, *89*, 90
Thermo King 74–5
Thurber, James 58
To Secure These Rights 26
toilets 56
Tom Mix 84
Toscanini, Arturo 82, 90
toys 61
train sets 61, *61*
transistors 75
travel 126–39
Treacy, Jack 57, 58
Trendle, George W. 84
Trigère, Pauline 103, *103*
Truman, Harry S. 21, 23, 26, 140
employment 64
Hawaii 25
housing 47
Indian Claims Commission 26, *26*
"Loyalty Program" 27
radio 87
sport 108
strikes 64–5
television 79
Tupper, Earl 54
Tupperware 54
Twain, Mark 24

typewriters 73

unions 64–5
United Nations 20–1, *21*

vacations 126–31
"Victory Garden" scheme 60
Vidal, Gore 120
Voss, Kay 10

Wagner-Steagall National Housing Act 1937 46–7
Walgreen, Charles R. Sr. 32
Walter, Bruno 123, *123*
Ward, Montgomery 39
Warner, Edward 138
Warner, Harry 100
Warshaw, Sam *119*
washing machines 54
Weill, Kurt 123
Welles, Orson 25, 85, 98, *99*
Westinghouse *54–5*, 93
"Wherry" homes 51
White Castle hamburger chain 43
Wilder, Billy 100
Wilkie, Wendell 140
Williams, Tennessee 117
Winchell, Walter 23, 87
Wise, Brownie 54
women
employment 16–17, 65, 68–70
fashion 102–3
Women In Defense 16
Woolworth, F. W. 32
Woolworths 32, *33*
Wurlitzer jukeboxes *96*
Wyatt, Wilson W. *47*
Wynn, Ed 89

Yalta conference 20–1, *20*
Yeatman, R.J. 140
Your Hit Parade 113

Bibliography

Albrecht, Donald (ed.): *World War II and the American Dream* (National Building Museum/MIT Press, 1995)

Aron, Cindy S.: *Working At Play—A History of Vacations in the United States* (Oxford University Press, 1999)

Basie, Count (with Murray, Albert): *Good Morning Blues* (Paladin, 1987)

Baudot, François: *A Century of Fashion* (Thames & Hudson, 1999)

Brogan, Hugh: *The Penguin History of the U.S.A.* (new edition) (Penguin, 2001)

Brokaw, Tom: *The Greatest Generation Speaks* (Random House, 1999)

Brooke-Ball, Peter: *The Great Fights* (Southwater, 2001)

Cooke, Alistair: *Alistair Cooke's America* (BBC, 1974)

Crawford, Richard: *America's Musical Life—A History* (W.W. Norton, 2001)

Crump, Spencer: *Route 66—America's First Main Street* (Zeta, 1996)

Eisenhower, John S.D.: *Allies—Pearl Harbor to D-Day* (Doubleday, 1982)

Evans, Harold: *The American Century* (Jonathan Cape, 1998)

Fleischhauer, Carl, and Brannan, Beverly W. (ed.): *Documenting America, 1935–1943* (University of California Press, 1988)

Fogelson, Robert M.: *Downtown—Its Rise and Fall, 1880–1950* (Yale University Press, 2001)

Freeth, Nick: *Route 66 – Main Street U.S.A.* (MBI, 2001)

George, Nelson: *The Death of Rhythm & Blues* (Omnibus Press, 1989)

Gillett, Charlie: *The Sound of the City* (third edition) (Souvenir Press, 1996)

Gunther, John: *Inside U.S.A.* (50th anniversary edition) (Curtis Publishing Company, 1947/New Press, 1997)

Halpert, Sam: *A Real Good War* (Southern Heritage Press, 1997)

Heimann, Jim (ed.): *40s—All American Ads* (Taschen, 2001)

Heimann, Jim: *Car Hops and Curb Service—A History of American Drive-In Restaurants 1920–1960* (Chronicle, 1996)

Heyman, Therese Thau: *Posters American Style* (NMAA, Smithsonian Institution/Abradale Press, 1998)

Heyworth, Peter (ed.): *Conversations with Klemperer* (Victor Gollancz, 1973)

Honig, Donald: *Baseball When The Grass Was Real* (Bison Books, 1993)

Jackson, Kenneth T.: *Crabgrass Frontier: The Suburbanization of the United States* (Oxford University Press, 1985)

Kemp, Tom: *The Climax of Capitalism—The U.S. Economy in the Twentieth Century* (Longman, 1990)

Kennedy, David M.: *Freedom From Fear—The American People in Depression and War, 1929–1945* (Oxford University Press, 1999)

Kotkin, Joel, and Grabowicz, Paul: *California Inc.* (Avon, 1982)

Lehmann, Nicholas: *Out of the Forties* (Fireside, 1985)

Lewis, Sinclair: *Main Street* (Penguin Putnam Inc., 1998)

Malone, Bill C.: *Country Music U.S.A.* (revised edition) (University of Texas Press, 1985)

Maupin, Armistead: *Tales of the City* (Chatto & Windus, 1989)

Okrent, Daniel, and Lewine, Harris: *The Ultimate Baseball Book* (Houghton Mifflin, 1991)

Palladino, Grace: *Teenagers—An American History* (BasicBooks, 1996)

Patterson, James T.: *Grand Expectations—The United States, 1945–1974* (Oxford University Press, 1996)

Schonberg, Harold C.: *The Lives of the Great Composers* (Abacus, 1992)

Schönberger, Angela (ed.): *Raymond Loewy—Pioneer of American Industrial Design* (Prestel, 1990)

Simon, George T.: *The Big Bands* (4th edition) (Schirmer, 1981)

Toland, John: *Infamy—Pearl Harbor and its Aftermath* (Methuen, 1982)

Urdang, Laurence (ed.): *The Timetables of American History* (updated edition) (Touchstone, 1996)

Walker, John (ed.): *Halliwell's Film & Video Guide 2001* (HarperCollins, 2000)

Acknowledgments

The author would like to thank Bill Harris, Don Judd, Mike Conroy, and the staff of the British Library and Barbican Library for their help and advice, and also Caroline Eley for compiling the index.

Two excerpts on pages 126–27 from *Working at Play—A History of Vacations in the United States* by Cindy S. Aron, published by Oxford University Press © Cindy S. Aron 1999.

One excerpt on page 116 from *"Many Happy Returns,"* from W.H. Auden: *The Collected Poems* by W.H. Auden, copyright © 1976 by Edward Mendelson, William Meredith, and Monroe K. Spears, Executors of the Estate of W.H. Auden. Used by permission of Random House, Inc. and Faber and Faber Ltd.

One excerpt on page 83 from *Good Morning Blues* by Count Basie (with Albert Murray), published by Da Capo Press, Perseus Books Group © Albert Murray and Count Basie Productions 1985.

Two excerpts on pages 10 and 23 from *The Greatest Generation Speaks* by Tom Brokaw © Tom Brokaw 1999.

One excerpt on page 78 from *The Best of Frasier,* published by Channel 4 Books (Macmillan), taken from *"Ham Radio,"* episode #40570-089, written by David Lloyd, created and developed by David Angell, Peter Casey, and David Lee, first transmitted in 1996 © Paramount Pictures 1999.

One excerpt on page 75 from *Fire in the Valley: The Making of the Personal Computer,* published by McGraw-Hill © 2000 Paul Freiberger and Michael Swaine, reprinted by permission of The McGraw-Hill Companies.

Two excerpts on page 36 from page 136 from *"A Supermarket in California,"* from *Collected Poems 1947–1980* by Allen Ginsberg, copyright © 1955 by Allen Ginsberg. Reprinted by permission of HarperCollins Publishers Inc.

One excerpt on page 96 from *From Blues to Bop,* ed. Richard N. Albert, published by Anchor Books (Doubleday) © 1990 Louisiana State University Press; original story © 1947 Elliot Grennard, renewed 1975 by the Estate of Elliot Grennard.

One excerpt on page 46 from *Home* by Edgar A. Guest, published by Reilly & Lee 1916.

Excerpts on pages 27, 31, 49, and 66 from *Inside U.S.A.* by John Gunther, published by The New Press © John Gunther 1946, 1947.

One excerpt on page 126 from *Mountain Greenery,* lyrics by Lorenz Hart, from the 1926 show *The Garrick Gaieties* © 1926 Warner Bros. Inc., Williamson Music, New York.

One excerpt on page 106 from *Baseball When The Grass Was Real,* published by Bison Books, University of Nebraska Press © Donald Honig 1975.

One excerpt on page 96 from *Saturday Night Fish Fry,* words and music by Ellis Walsh and Louis Jordan, copyright 1949 (renewed) CHERIO CORP. All rights reserved.

Two excerpts on pages 13 and 47 from *Freedom From Fear* by David M. Kennedy, published by Oxford University Press © David M. Kennedy 1999.

Excerpts on pages 30–31 and 40 from *Main Street: The Story of Carol Kennicott,* copyright 1920 by Harcourt, Inc. and reviewed 1948 by Sinclair Lewis, Harcourt, Inc.

One excerpt on page 48 from *Acres and Pains* by S.J. Perelman, taken from *Most of the Most of S.J. Perelman* (anthology), published by Random House, Inc. and Methuen Publishing Limited © S.J. Perelman, reprinted by permission.

Excerpts on page 56 from *The Specialist* by Charles Sale, published by Putnam & Company Ltd 1930.

One excerpt on page 58 from *The Thurber Carnival* by James Thurber, published by Penguin Books Ltd 1953.

One excerpt on page 140 from *One World* by Wendell Willkie, published by Cassell & Co. 1943.

The publishers gratefully acknowledge permission to reproduce copyright material. Every effort has been made to contract original sources and copyright holders for permissions. In case of any omissions, please contact Salamander Books Ltd.

Picture Credits

L=left; R=right; T=top; B=bottom; F=far; M=middle

Advertising Archives: Front cover L and 49L, back cover R and 52, 54, 56BL/BR, 59BL, 75TR, 79B, 90, 96, 130BR, 136BL, 138

Association of American Railroads/Boston & Maine: 130B

Corbis: Front flap T and page 1, front cover ML and 10, back cover L, 11, 15BR, 16R, 18–19, 21B, 22BR, 26T, 38BR, 39, 40TR, 41B, 43TR, 47T, 50–51, 53, 59BR, 61, 64–65, 74BL 75TR, 76–77, 85, 87, 91, 92B, 93, 102L, 103B 104BL, 105BR, 110, 111T, 112BR, 114–15, 122, 123BR, 139

Driggs Collection: 83B

Courtesy of the General Mills Archives: 55L

Hulton Archive: Front flap B and 8, back flap T and 82BL, back flap B and 58, front cover FL and 43TL, front cover MR and 79T, front cover R and 14/Norman Rockwell, front cover FR and 55, main picture back cover, back cover FL and 33B, back cover ML and 38T, back cover FR and 41TR, 6–7, 8, 12, 13, 15TL, 16L, 17, 20, 21T, 23, 25, 26B, 27R, 31, 32TR, 32B, 33TR, 34–35B, 35, 37, 42, 43BL, 44–45, 46, 47B, 48, 49R, 54–55, 57, 60–61, 62–63, 66–67, 68–69, 72–73, 80–81, 82–83, 83TL, 84, 86, 88–89, 94–95, 97, 99, 100–01, 102R, 103T, 106, 108, 109, 111B, 112 and BL, 116–17, 118BR, 119, 120–21, 123L, 124–25, 126–27, 131, 136TR, 137, 141,

The Kobal Collection: 98

Library of Congress: LC-USF 34-53307–D Marion Post Wolcott main picture front cover and 28–29, LC-USW3T01-17782-E 59T

Oldsmobile History Center: 134T, 135TL

Minnesota Historical Society: 30, 32B, 40B

National African American Museum and Cultural Center: 107B

National Archives: 49-6800 105TL; 50-9473 107TL

J.C. Penney: 38BL

Special Collections: Photographic Archives, University of Louisville: 70–71, 132–33

Neil Sutherland/Chrysalis Images: 34–35T, 41TL/BL, 111M

Syracuse University: 22BL, 48M